They Did It the Hard Way

Garry Hogg

THEY DID IT THE HARD WAY

Seven Astounding Journeys

Pantheon Books

Copyright © 1973 by Garry Hogg
All rights reserved under International and Pan-American Copyright Conventions. Published in the United States by Pantheon Books, a division of Random House, Inc. Originally published in Great Britain by Abelard-Schuman, Ltd., London.

Library of Congress Cataloging in Publication Data
Hogg, Garry. They did it the hard way.

  Summary: Seven true adventure stories of people who by choice or necessity made arduous expeditions through desolate places, sometimes totally dependent on their endurance for survival.

  1. Adventure and adventures—Juvenile literature.
  2. Voyages and travel—Juvenile literature.
  [1. Adventure and adventurers. 2. Voyages and travels] I. Title.
  G525.H79 910′.92′2 [B] 72-7624
  ISBN 0-394-82602-7 ISBN 0-394-92601-1 (lib. bdg.)

Manufactured in the United States of America

Contents

Foreword	ix
Douglas Mawson in Antarctica	3
Wilfred P. Thesiger in the Empty Quarter	27
Peter Fleming in the Brazilian Jungle	53
Dervla Murphy from Ireland to India	78
John Hillaby in Search of Lake Rudolf	100
André Migot in Bandit Country	123
Laurens van der Post in Nyasaland	147

Maps

Mawson's estimated route	4
Thesiger's route in The Empty Quarter	28
Fleming's route in Brazil	54
Dervla Murphy's route from Ireland to India	80
Hillaby's route to Lake Rudolf	102
Migot's route from Kunming to Koko Nor	124
Van der Post's route in Nyasaland	148

Foreword

The era of great overland journeys on foot virtually came to an end with the passing of the nineteenth century, except perhaps for those in the Arctic and Antarctic. It had been the age of incredible cross-country treks in search of gold in the Klondike and elsewhere—those made by the "Forty-niners" and their successors. It had been the period during which Australia was opened up by pioneers on foot like Robert O'Hara Burke and William J. Wills, who were the first men to cross the huge continent from south to north, all of whom performed fantastic feats of courage, pertinacity and fortitude in their determination to press on beyond the known frontiers of the land in order to find out "what lies beyond." All of them achieved what they did achieve "the hard way," for their expeditions were all mounted before the era of mechanized vehicles, of air-cover and of radio communication.

As the decades succeeded one another after the turn of the century, more and more explorers-by-land came to depend on vehicles expressly designed for their specialized needs. There were "Weasels" and "Sno-cats," mechanized sleds, and there were planes that could land and take off on ice and water as well as dry land. These of course enabled some spectacular journeys of discovery and exploration to be made. But somehow—though perhaps members of those expeditions might not entirely agree!—this diminished the caliber of the men who undertook them. Modern machinery had to a large extent replaced the sheer muscle that had been the motivating power of men who, in that earlier century, had covered hundreds, even thousands, of arduous

Foreword

miles with nothing to depend on other than their own strength and stamina.

There were, of course, exceptions. In the past half-century men like Nansen and Sven Hedin explored the Arctic and the Gobi Desert; P. H. Newby walked in the Hindu Kush; Freya Stark wintered in Arabia; Harold Elvin cycled to Chandigarh; Knud Rasmussen took a dog-sled team from Hudson Bay across the North American continent to the Bering Strait; Sir Martin Lindsay did a notable journey on foot through the Ituri Forest and the Belgian Congo; Beryl Miles slept out beneath the Australian skies; the Frenchman Périot covered 1,500 miles on foot through Liberia; and as recently as 1968–9 Wally Herbert led a party on foot across the North Pole from Alaska to Spitzbergen, a marathon trek that lasted no less than 476 days. And these are not by any means all the examples of men (and women too) who in recent years chose to do their journeys the hard way, as the following chapters will show.

The seven notable journeys that constitute this book were not in any sense attempts to smash existing records or even to set up an initial record. They were all undertaken either because the man (or in one case the woman) had a deep-rooted desire to undertake such an expedition without the obvious advantages of modern mechanical equipment, or because the journey had been commissioned by some authority and could not be carried out in any other way because there was no equipment available that could have matched the demands likely to be made on it.

These journeys all reveal two important facts: that the human spirit is the most vital piece of equipment in any enterprise, whether on a large scale or on a small one. And that the elements of courage, fortitude, initiative, endurance and faith are as strong today, in this second half of the twentieth century, as they were a hundred years ago when there was little else that a man could depend upon to achieve his objective—when he had no option but to do it the hard way.

They Did It the Hard Way

Douglas Mawson in Antarctica

A twenty-eight-year-old engineer and scientist, Douglas Mawson, can claim to have been the youngest man ever to lead a party of explorers in the frozen continent of Antarctica. The Australasian Antarctic Expedition, of which he was the leader, was itself a party of twenty-odd young men. It started with high hopes in 1912. It was hit by tragedy, but demonstrated what courage and pertinacity and true faith could accomplish in the face of almost unbelievable odds.

Today—as may be seen, for example, in the notable crossing of Antarctica by Fuchs and Hillary a few years ago—men have at their disposal the enormous advantages of mechanization. They have the invaluable "Sno-cat," and other mechanically-propelled vehicles specifically designed for use in such conditions. They have air cover from the American base close to the South Pole. They are in constant communication by radio transmission with bases from which, in an emergency, practical assistance is readily forthcoming. Mawson and his men had no such facilities. What they set out to do, they did the hard way.

Mawson's party was put ashore by Captain Davis of the *Aurora* in a bay in Adélie Land to which they gave the name Commonwealth Bay. The point at which they landed, close to Cape Denison—named after one of the Australian sponsors of the expedition—lay on longitude 140E, some two thousand miles due south of Adelaide, in Southern Australia. Here the men constructed their Main Base, from building materials unloaded together with vast quantities of

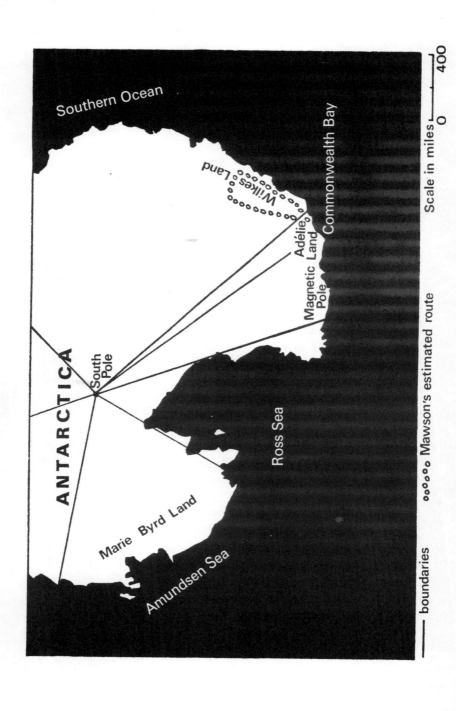

stores, before the ship turned for home. The date when they bade Captain Davis farewell and began to fend for themselves was in February 1912.

Like all pioneers, whether preparing to climb high mountains or exploring deserts or other little-known territory, the party spent some time, not merely establishing their base but acclimatizing themselves to the rigorous conditions that are found in Adélie Land. Temperatures were lower than any of these men had previously experienced, but they had come prepared for them. What they had not anticipated was the tremendous force of the prevailing winds, for which Adélie Land has come to be notorious. The combination of intense cold and furious and incessant gales made the erection of the huts for their meteorological instruments—their anemometers, anemographs and other equipment that had to be exposed to the elements—a task that called for herculean effort and immense and sustained will-power.

To prepare themselves physically for the surveying trips, the main objectives of the expedition, they embarked on journeys of ever-increasing length and difficulty across the ice. These were spread over a period of several months, for Mawson was not one to take risks by being impetuous or over-confident. In November, however, he decided that the time was ripe for a start to be made on their major projects. He divided his men into six small parties, each of which was to fulfill a specific objective. One was to make a survey of the South Pole Magnetic Pole area, south-south-east of Cape Denison and south of Mt. Murchison. Another was to explore the coastline westward of Main Base. A third was to survey the coastline eastward.

The most important of the individual survey treks to be undertaken was also to be eastward, but a good deal farther inland. Mawson anticipated that this would prove the most arduous and exacting of all, and for this reason, as leader, he undertook it himself. He chose two men to accompany him, men on whom he knew he could rely implicitly whatever degree of hardship or danger they might encounter. One of these was Dr. Xavier Mertz, the other was a youthful giant of a man, Lieutenant B. E. S. Ninnis. Little did he dream, when he selected Ninnis as one of his two companions, that this man's very stature and weight would prove to be the cause of the first real disaster that befell what he named his Far Eastern Party.

The six parties went their several ways on November 17th. As Mawson and his party were undertaking the longest and most strenuous of the treks across the ice, they set out with two sleds, each hauled by a small team of willing huskies. Mawson took charge of one of these, the other was handled alternately by Ninnis and Mertz. Whichever man was not controlling the sled went ahead on skis to pick out the most promising route among the crevasses and "sastrugi" —the irregularly shaped "reefs" of piled-up ice resulting from the gales and changes of temperature, not unlike desert sand dunes, but of course jagged and infinitely more formidable to negotiate.

To begin with, in spite of the weather conditions, they made fair progress. For some miles the ice was so smooth that the men had to apply the sled brakes to prevent their overrunning the dog-teams when they were crossing a downward slope. But there were later days when the weather deteriorated and they were forced to pitch their small tent and remain in their sleeping-bags until the storm blew itself out. One of these storms lasted for three days and nights without a break. It called for true devotion to duty, not to say courage, to creep out of sleeping-bag and tent to go and feed the huskies, lying curled up nose to tail like giant hedgehogs but ravenous for food all the same.

There were days when they covered as much as fifteen or even twenty miles between striking camp and pitching their tent at the end of the day's march. There were other days when the crevasses they encountered in their path were so numerous, and so difficult to negotiate, that four or five miles could be regarded as something of a triumph. Ten miles a day, Mawson recorded in his diary, could be regarded as a good average run. On December 14th, just one month after saying goodbye to the other parties, he estimated that his own party had covered something over three hundred miles, and in so doing had surveyed and charted a substantial area in this corner of Adélie Land.

The usual order of travel was first either Ninnis or Mertz, on skis, ranging ahead to pick the route. Next came Mawson, with the smaller of the two sleds. Bringing up the rear was either Mertz or Ninnis with the larger sled. There was a reason for this. Mawson held that the safest place in the line was the last, for those ahead of the big sled could satisfy themselves that the surface, especially near the crevasses, their main worry, was strong enough to bear them all. If one of these should collapse, the big sled, carrying their main supplies, would be kept clear of the danger spot by its driver until a safer route had been located. It was sound reasoning —unhappily it was a plan that was not foolproof.

On December 14th Mertz, far in the lead on his skis, halted and sent back the agreed signal: DANGER—CREVASSE. Mawson passed the signal back to Ninnis, in the rear with the big sled. He then went cautiously ahead with his own smaller one until he had drawn level with Mertz. The first thing he did was to work out from his tables the exact position and record it on his chart. Then he and Mertz did a reconnaissance, and Mawson came to the conclusion that the crevasse could be crossed safely provided this was done, as is customary, in a diagonal direction. He whipped up his dog-team, called upon them for a spurt, and a matter of seconds later was safe on the far side. There he halted and signaled to Ninnis to follow his example.

Ninnis whipped up his dog-team and approached the edge of the crevasse at a brisk rate. The icy silence of the waste was broken by the hiss of runners and the lusty breathing of the huskies. Then, suddenly, there was a new sound—a strangled cry from Xavier Mertz. Mawson swung around, and was just in time to see the tail end of the big sled vanish into the crevasse which he had so recently negotiated. The snow-bridge over it had collapsed under the combined weight of the big sled and its young giant of a driver who, instead of riding it, as he should have done, had been running alongside it, his massive weight carried not by the sled runners but by his own two feet, which of course did not distribute the weight as the runners did. They had plunged through the packed snow forming the "lid" of the crevasse, and the sled had vanished through it.

Horrified, Mawson and Mertz worked their way cautiously back along their own tracks in the snow-covered ice, dreading what they would find. As they came close to the near side of the crevasse they could hear a muffled whimpering, as of a dog in pain. Uncoiling a length of rope as they did so, they approached the very edge of the crevasse. To the right and left of them there was a narrow, almost hairline crack in the surface. Immediately in front of them there was a gaping hole at least ten feet wide, with a jagged edge showing all too clearly how the relatively thin covering of packed snow and ice had been broken through.

Mawson lowered himself to the surface and inched his way forward. He had looped one end of the rope around his waist and Mertz was holding the other, paying out the rope a foot at a time and keeping it very nearly taut. Mawson looked sheer down into the crevasse which was lit by a sinister greenish light to a depth of more than a hundred feet—a hundred feet of glass-smooth ice, down which a scar ran as far as a sort of ice shelf that was just within view. On the shelf lay a husky, in a posture so contorted that it was quite evident its back had been broken by the fall. Wedged across the narrowing width of the crevasse a few yards farther down was the sled, from which the cargo had broken loose and was dangling at the end of its lashings. Of Lieutenant Ninnis and the other huskies there was no sign whatsoever.

The whimpering ceased, and all now was silence. Though he knew it was futile, Mawson cupped his lips and yelled downward into the unseen depths of the crevasse. There was no response. He yelled again, and yet again, in the vain hope that his companion might only have been stunned, his fall broken somehow, that he might, by an even greater miracle, be hauled alive out of the crevasse. But with every succeeding minute he knew that it was a forlorn hope.

Stunned with shock and grief, Xavier Mertz and his leader remained at the edge of the crevasse, unwilling still to relinquish hope. But at the close of that long and terrible day there was no hope left. Mawson read a makeshift version of the Burial Service there in the icy waste. Then, without speaking to one another, their hearts full of grief, they turned their faces away from the crevasse, the grave of their companion, to consider what next to do. From now on they were two on their own.

One thing at least was certain—they must turn around immediately and make for Main Base. Almost all their provisions had been lost with the big sled, so they could not afford to remain on trek a day longer than was absolutely necessary. Taking careful stock of what remained to them on the smaller sled, Mawson estimated that there was sufficient—just—to sustain the two of them for ten days. But this would mean that they must restrict themselves to a daily ration so small it would hardly enable them to maintain their strength and resistance to the bitter cold. It had taken them three times as long, with two sleds, to do the outward journey, and they had been a team of three men, seasoned, fit and well equipped. Now they were but two men, already feeling the effects of their three-hundred-mile trek. They had no tent for protection at night or especially bad weather conditions and the greater part of their food was gone. Their situation was grim indeed.

With heavy hearts, the two men turned about, to face a three-hundred-mile trek in appalling conditions. There was little food for their dog-team. But, ironically enough, in their dog-team lay part of their hope of survival after ten days were past. A dog could be killed, and its flesh, horrible as the thought was, could be eaten both by man and by beast. Polar explorers had been reduced to this expedient before, and what others had done, Mawson and Mertz, in the last resort, could also do.

By the end of December, two weeks after the death of Lieutenant Ninnis, the first dog had been killed and its flesh eaten, supplemented by a handful of raisins and a mouthful or two of precious chocolate. The flesh was hard and stringy, for huskies are sheer bundles of muscle when in good health, without an ounce of spare fat on them. But the depleted team was already showing signs of losing condition. It was obvious that soon they would be unable to haul the sled any farther. They would then serve no purpose except as food. But there was a limit to the quantity of this that could be carried when the sled had to be manhandled instead of being hauled by the dog-team. Mawson and Mertz were now eating at most three-quarters of a pound of mixed and generally very unappetizing food per day. It was not enough to keep out the cold, let alone give them the necessary strength to supplement the efforts of the diminished team.

As day succeeded day, their rate of progress became slower and slower. On the last day of December they covered, with their best efforts, less than three miles in all. Mawson noticed that his companion was showing signs of distress, though he was doing his best to conceal them. Asked how he felt, Mertz confessed that for some time he had been suffering from almost unbearable stomach pains.

He put these down to the unsavory and unpalatable dog's meat on which they were now subsisting. With typical generosity, Mawson made over to him his own pitifully small ration of chocolate and raisins and told him to eat no more meat until the pains subsided. As a matter of fact he himself was suffering in the same way, but as leader was determined not to admit to this lest the news further depress his companion.

During the first week in January weather conditions deteriorated rapidly. Heavy snow began to fall. A dark, overcast sky and a mounting wind, driving the snow blindingly in their faces, made travel on foot over treacherous ground and extensive areas of sastrugi almost impossible. Time and again they were forced to come to a halt, rig a makeshift shelter which was in fact nothing more than a piece of canvas rigged on a pair of skis erected to windward of them, and wriggle into their sleeping-bags. Providentially, these had been carried on the smaller of the two sleds, or they, like the tent, would have been lost in the crevasse. But because of the lack of true shelter, the sleeping-bags themselves were almost continuously wet. Partly as a result of this, in the second week of January it was found that Mertz was suffering not only from stomach cramps and other pains, but from frostbite—an affliction for which, in such conditions, there was no cure whatsoever.

Disasters rarely come singly, and Mawson by now suspected that Fate had not yet finished with them. He was right. Their daily average was now down to no more than two or three miles. Mertz was a very sick man indeed. He had recurrent spasms that seemed almost like minor epileptic fits, and during these Mawson had to lash him in his sleeping-bag and watch over him like a sick child. He admitted in his diary that this responsibility, on top of his own very considerable pain and exhaustion, lessened their chances of survival with every passing hour on the trek.

On the 6th and 7th of January Mertz lay in a coma,

which alternated with violent movements accompanied by delirious ravings. In the afternoon of the second day Mawson, now completely exhausted by his vigil, dropped off into a deep sleep. When he awoke some hours later, chilled to the bone and racked with cramps in both legs and arms, his immediate concern, as always, was for his sick companion. But Mertz was now past needing attention. Mercifully, he had died in his sleep. Mawson touched him and found him ice-cold and rigid. For him, this "man of character, generous and of noble parts," as his leader referred to Xavier Mertz, the Antarctic trek had ended.

Now, Mawson was absolutely alone. The last of the huskies had had to be killed and eaten for food—food that far from sustaining life in his companion seemed to have contributed to his death. The sled was too heavy to be hauled by one man. Mawson set to work and cut it in two. Onto the forward half he loaded the absolutely vital items of food and clothing remaining to him, reducing this to a weight which he felt he could haul single-handed across the ice. The other end of the sled was stood on end to mark the spot where he had buried Mertz.

He calculated that more than a hundred miles lay between the burial place and the security and companionship he longed for, but hardly dared to hope for, at Main Base. Every day, every hour, counted more than ever. But Fate intervened once again—weather conditions deteriorated to such an extent that he could not even begin this last, lonely stage of his trek. He must find shelter behind the improvised windbreak, close to Mertz's grave, and wait for conditions to improve—if they ever did. Not daring to believe that he would complete this Far Eastern Survey, he wrote up what he could of it in his diary, and prepared to sit out the blizzard as best he could.

On January 11th, four days after Mertz's death, the weather, though still shockingly bad, improved sufficiently for him to feel that he could make a fresh start. So now began one of the most terrible journeys any man has ever undertaken, and survived, either with a companion or alone —and Douglas Mawson was very much alone.

Within less than an hour he realized that something was very wrong with his feet. They not only felt sore—an experience he was by now well accustomed to—but they felt as though the soles were somehow detached from the rest of his feet. Puzzled, he sat down on the ice and carefully removed first one boot and then the other. He was shocked by what examination revealed. He found that the sole of each foot had, quite literally, become separated from the rest of the foot. It resembled a thick, leather-like, foot-shaped strip of flesh, like an inner sole, detached from the rest of the flesh by a thin layer of jelly-like fluid that had oozed out into his woolen socks and spread into his boots. Beneath this was newly-forming skin, soft as that of a baby and extremely tender to the touch. It was with feet in this condition that he faced a march over rough ice and snow, hauling a sled single-handed, for at least a hundred exhausting miles.

Delving into his precious medicine chest, which fortunately had been carried on the smaller sled, he found some lanolin, an ointment carried by all mountaineers and explorers whose flesh must be exposed to extremes of heat and cold. With this he smeared the newly-forming skin. Then he replaced the separated skin soles and bound them to his feet with bandages as best he could. Finally he put on all the spare socks he possessed, and with his feet thus encased, thrust them painfully into his fur-lined boots. It was the best he could do, and must suffice.

Encouraged by a break in the vicious weather, and aware that had he performed this operation on his feet in the sort of weather he had been experiencing for many days past, he would certainly have been afflicted by frostbite, he set off once more in surprisingly good heart. But so painful were his feet, in spite of their doctoring, that by eight o'clock that evening he had covered less than five miles. Having made camp, he gingerly examined his feet again. They had stood up better than he expected to the strain of sled hauling, though there was blood as well as fluid and discolored lanolin inside his socks and boots. He noted in his diary that the date was January 13th. He gave no indication that he was suspicious regarding that ominous figure, but simply wrote in his diary: "Things look bad, but I shall persevere."

Four days later he came within an inch of final disaster. Perhaps because his feet were less sensitive, in one respect, to the prevailing conditions, he stepped onto a patch of soft snow that was in fact the thin covering of an unseen crevasse. In less time than it takes to tell what happened, he found himself falling down through a blanket of soft, powdery snow and in almost complete darkness. Fortunately he had roped himself to the sled he was hauling, and in spite of the suddenness of the accident had time to realize that his downward motion was slowing, the sled acting as a brake. Even as he dangled there at the end of the harness, he speculated as to whether the sled would reach the lip of the crevasse, topple over and kill him by its sheer weight as it fell vertically down on him.

Strangely, the sled came to a halt, its runners balked by a build-up of soft snow, right on the brink. Mawson found himself revolving slowly at the end of the rope, some twenty feet below the surface. He could see the forward end of the sled almost immediately above him. He estimated the width of the crevasse at about six feet. Its sides were sheer, glass-smooth, so there was no hope whatsoever of being able to climb back up them to the opening. But some six feet or so above his head there happened to be a knot in the rope. He made a superhuman effort and somehow succeeded in struggling up the rope until he could grasp it. He paused to get his breath and then, by a further superhuman effort, which he hardly believed himself capable of, got his feet onto the knot and so was able to reach up and grasp a second knot a yard or so higher up still. By repeating the process he managed at last to spread his arms outward over what remained of the snow lid. But just as he thought he was about to break free, his foot slipped and the weight thrown on the snow broke it further. Once again he found himself dangling at the full length of the rope up which he had so laboriously climbed.

For the first time, as he was to admit later, he not only believed that death was now inevitable, but found himself half wishing that the end might come quickly. Racked by stomach pains, with his feet causing him agony, his body gripped in the noose of rope, its pressure increased by the fact that every pocket and fold of his garments had become filled with loose snow, his hands numb with cold, he heard himself saying that to cut himself free of the harness and plummet into the darkness below his feet would simply be a merciful relief.

Possibly the very thought that he had almost welcomed death frightened him more than the situation in which he now found himself. Anyway, a wave of determination swept through him. He found himself momentarily possessed of what he could recognize even in his present agony of body and mind as truly superhuman strength. He reached once again for the nearest knot in the rope, seized it with an iron grip and hauled himself upward until he could grip it between his knees. He took a fresh grip, got his feet onto the knot and reached for the next one, several feet higher still, as he had done before.

But this time, by some contortion which, he said afterward, he would have believed only a trained acrobat could have achieved, he reversed his position on the rope and succeeded in actually *pushing* himself up the last yard and a half, so that his feet and legs emerged from the crevasse before his head. He bent his legs and rested them cautiously, experimentally, on the lip of the crevasse. Then, forcing himself upward a few inches at a time, he found that he could distribute his weight in such a fashion as not to lay any one part of it too heavily on the fragile snow. Eventually he emerged completely. He had just sufficient strength left to reach for the broken sled and with its help as an anchor, haul himself clear of the crevasse. Then he hauled the sled clear and rolled onto it. There he passed out, utterly exhausted, having saved his life by a maneuver that astonished him afterward whenever he thought about it.

Exhausted and half frozen as he was, it was a long time before he felt able to make a fresh start. As he lay there, slowly recovering his strength, he tried to work out a system by which he might hope to avoid a repetition of the accident that had so nearly resulted in his death. There would, he knew well, be more crevasses to negotiate. He must take better precautions against falling victim to them. He decided to make a rope ladder out of some of the Alpine-type rope he had with him. One end of this he secured firmly to the front of his sled, the other was slung over his shoulder and linked to the sled harness. If he was unfortunate enough to fall into another crevasse, he told himself, he might be able to climb back up this ladder. It would be easier than swarming up a single knotted rope.

He hardly dared believe, though, that he would have the resources of strength and stamina to perform this feat yet again. And of course next time the sled itself might fall into the crevasse after him, as it had done with poor Lieutenant Ninnis. He was realist enough to recognize the inescapable fact that if this were to happen—and, miraculously, it had not happened to him the last time—then all would truly be over with him.

Within a few hours, as it turned out, he was able to put his new device to the test. On January 19th, in spite of driving snow and the resultant darkness which, as he recorded, "coralled me in," he determined to continue his interminable trek, "leaving the outcome to Providence." His feet were intensely painful and he now suspected the onset of frostbite in one of them, if not both. All strength seemed to have gone out of his legs. He found himself staggering from one foot to the other like a sailor on a heaving deck. As a result, he placed his feet clumsily instead of treading carefully.

An hour after setting out, dragging his sled behind him, one foot plunged clean through the snow covering of a crevasse which was camouflaged by the loose snow falling in the blizzard. He went straight through it, and had just time to think, as a man does before drowning, "this must be the end." But once again Providence favored him. The sled jammed across the top of the crevasse, which was a narrow one, and securely anchored him. Carefully, fearful of dislodging it, he swiveled around until he could place one foot on the bottom rung of his improvised ladder. With infinite caution he climbed, one slow step at a time, until at last he could reach out and grasp the curved sled runner itself. A moment later he had scrambled clear. Once again he threw himself onto the sled, and breathing a sigh of relief and thankfulness for his escape, passed out from sheer exhaustion.

When he awoke, he found that he had emerged into a blizzard that had, if anything, increased in ferocity. Still exhausted, and affected no doubt by delayed shock at his near escape from death, Mawson rigged his canvas shelter and made himself as comfortable as possible in the circumstances, hoping to wear the blizzard out by his patience. He knew, as he crouched there, that with every day, every hour, spent in this way his pitifully small resources of food were running lower and lower. He could not afford to let an hour go by without some attempt at progress in the direction of Main Base. But in this blinding, frozen darkness, further progress was impossible—to continue would be suicidal.

The first stroke of what could be called luck came his way when, unexpectedly but to his enormous relief, the wind direction suddenly shifted from west to east. Now, for a while at any rate, instead of battling inch by strenuous inch in the teeth of a westerly gale sweeping over a huge expanse of Adélie Land, he found himself being bowled along by a powerful wind coming from the opposite direction altogether. It was so strong that at times, where the ice was smooth, the sled was thrown against his heels and he was tripped and sent sprawling. He had to rig a system of ropes so that he could control the sled from the side during these furious gusts. But at least in such conditions he was able to cover far more ground than had been possible for many days, even weeks, past.

As a result of this improvement in conditions Mawson began once again to believe that he might after all reach Main Base, instead of dying on the icy plateau of combined starvation and exposure. He may not have admitted to himself that this was what would probably be his ultimate fate, but it was only when he began at last to make some real progress that he realized how near he had come to accepting the inevitable.

He had hardly reached this new stage of slight optimism, however, when Fate struck once more. The wind that had been assisting him so generously dropped as suddenly as it had sprung up. As it dropped, the sheer weight of falling snow began to build up. It built up quite frighteningly. It filled the air, so that the lone traveler actually had to breathe snow. When he paused in his staggering stride to regain his breath, the snow built up all around his sled so that it became impossible to shift it. Not only that. So heavy was the falling snow that it built up around his boots, and he had to repeatedly lift each foot and plant it down firmly— and agonizingly—again to avoid being literally rooted to the spot. As for pitching his makeshift tent, he knew that if he once did that, and fell asleep behind its inadequate shelter, he would be entombed in a very short time by the ever-increasing weight of the snow.

So, he kept going as best he might. On one of his enforced stops he took stock of the food situation. It was worse than he had feared. He estimated that he now had barely two pounds of food left in all. It consisted mainly of dog's flesh that he managed somehow to eat in small quantities even though it had contributed to the death of his friend Xavier Mertz, a handful of raisins, a few precious fragments of chocolate, and a few crumbs of biscuit. That was all. Meanwhile he had lost track of the distances covered each day, for in such conditions it was impossible to estimate with any degree of accuracy what mileage he was achieving. It seemed to him—to judge by the painful and interminable effort expended—that he was covering huge distances, but he well knew that what felt like twenty miles could well be no more than two miles, or even less. At the time he buried Mertz he calculated that he still had a hundred miles ahead of him before he reached Main Base. It could be even more than that. How many of those endless miles still remained to be covered? There was no way of answering that bitter question. There was nothing to do but go on during such times as conditions made some sort of progress feasible, and to wait when further battling against them became impossible.

His strangely matter-of-fact acceptance of the inevitable was to pay off. On the morning of January 29th, after a whole day during which he had been blizzard-bound, he had struggled, by his estimate, a distance of four or perhaps five miles when first to his complete astonishment and then to his overwhelming delight he almost ran into a cairn of snow blocks that was, quite obviously, man made.

Feverishly, he broke into it. He found a small cache of food, together with a note to the effect that this had been placed there by three of his companions who had become increasingly worried about him after completing their own trek. They had returned to Main Base, but would set out again as soon as conditions of visibility made further search practicable. The note gave the welcome information that the cairn was just twenty-eight miles from the base.

The news was almost more welcome than the small supply of food. Short of actually encountering the search-party itself, this was the most wonderful thing Mawson could have dreamed of. Twenty-eight miles! Surely even with feet as agonizingly painful as they now were, he could cover those few remaining miles—only about a quarter of the total journey he had had to undertake alone after the tragic loss of his second companion?

There was some other news in the note. It was news that should give him encouragement as he slogged over the last remaining miles of icy waste. The Australasian Antarctic Expedition's relief ship had anchored offshore in Commonwealth Bay, within hailing distance of Main Base, where she had dropped them more than twelve months before. The ship was waiting for his return. Mawson tried to calculate how long it should take him to cover those last twenty-eight miles. At the rate of progress he had been making for the past good many days it would probably still be a long time, for physically he was now in very bad shape indeed. But thanks to the cache of food and, hardly less, to the knowledge that a search-party was on the lookout for him and might be encountered at any moment, he felt able to go ahead at his best speed.

But once again Fate intervened. The weather turned against him at the very moment when he was setting off on this last lap. The wind swung around and increased in strength as hour succeeded hour. The going was now icier than it had been during the heavy snowfall. Heading into the bitter wind, he could hardly keep his footing for two paces together. Time and again he stumbled as his feet slipped from beneath him. It was as though some malevolent being were clutching at them, determined to do everything in its power to impede his progress. Each time he struggled to his feet he felt weaker, less able to stand up to the ever-mounting pressure of the wind on his chest, now risen to gale force.

If only he had still possessed the invaluable crampons which he had used when they first set out, he might have had a chance. At least their steel "bite" on the ice would have enabled him to remain upright, plunging forward to gain a few yards between each brief halt and the next. But the crampons had been lost, with so much else that was important to him. The soles of his boots had long since worn smooth, as well as thin. As he put each one down it felt as though it was his naked foot, not a boot at all, that was being pressed onto the glacial surface.

Then snow began to fall once again, and to fall more and more heavily. The cold increased and the snow packed hard on the ice as soon as it touched it. He hoped that this less smooth surface might enable him to get a better grip. But the wind was by now so violent that it continuously swept the snow past him, tearing at his boots. Eventually, though he knew that even one halt might make the difference between disaster and salvation, he was forced to give up. He rigged his makeshift canvas windbreak and cowered down in the lee of it, praying that the gale and the snow that it carried in its teeth, which by now had increased to a true Antarctic blizzard, would let up.

It was while sheltering there that the idea came to him to try to construct a pair of crampons to fit onto the soles of his boots. Using fragments of material—two small pieces of wood from a box that contained his navigating equipment and a handful of nails—he constructed two crazy-looking crampons. These he laboriously fastened with twine to the soles of his boots. When at last he was able to continue on his way, it seemed as though he had solved this one at least among his many problems. They appeared to work. To begin with, at any rate. But the strain on them as he leaned forward into the gale, tugging his sled behind him, soon proved too great for them. One after another the nails he had driven through the pieces of wood, bent over and buckled into the wood itself. They served no further useful purpose, and only added weight to his dragging steps. Disappointed, he discarded them altogether.

He lost all count of time. The blizzard raged so continuously that he could no longer tell night from day. One thing only he knew—now that the general slope of the icy surface was downward he must be approaching the shore. And it was close to the shore that the huts constituting Main Base had been erected. Off that shore, their relief ship was awaiting his return. This downward trend, however, produced its own complications. The sled continually caught up with him, battering into the back of his painful feet, threatening to trip him and send him flying, threatening, even, to break away from him altogether, so that he would have lost the last remaining provisions and gear. Once again Mawson found himself wondering whether he would in fact make it back to base—and growled at himself for entertaining such pessimistic thoughts. The spirit, now, was stronger than the flesh.

His courage and faith were rewarded. One day, quite unexpectedly since he had ceased to be able to estimate the mileage covered between each enforced halt and the next, there hove suddenly into view, during a temporary lull in the blizzard, the beacon that one of the parties had erected outside a natural ice cave, to which they had jokingly given the name Aladdin's Cave. But for the brief lull in the blizzard he might have missed it altogether. It proved to be his salvation. Stumbling toward it, he was able to escape from the fury of the gale and snow into comparative calm. Searching eagerly, he spied another small cache of food. Among its basic contents was a rare luxury—three oranges and a pineapple.

Now Mawson knew that, barring something utterly unforeseen, he could consider himself safe. He was out of the furious blizzard. Aladdin's Cave was only five miles from Main Base. Nothing, surely, could prevent him from covering those last few miles. He could, if the worst came to the worst, abandon his sled. They could return to collect it when the blizzard eased. If absolutely necessary, he could do those last few miles on his hands and knees! Nothing, he repeated to himself, could prevent him from reaching Main Base.

But, for a while, at least, the ever-mounting blizzard could and did. Looking out from the comparative shelter of his ice cave, he could see, and without going to the painful expedient of testing it for himself, that the blizzard had greatly increased in force and intensity even during the brief hour he had rested and had a meal. He could see that it was worse than anything he had experienced in all the weeks he had been on his trek. If he had not reached Aladdin's Cave when he did, he would almost certainly have perished in it; to venture out into it would be sure death.

Then passed what was certainly the longest drawn-out and most frustrating week of his whole six-hundred-mile journey. For seven days and seven nights the blizzard raged. Try as he would to deny the evidence of his senses, he had to admit to himself that the blizzard's force was steadily increasing all the time. He was only five miles from Main Base—but it might have been five hundred, for all that he could do about it in such conditions. Very soon, he reminded himself, he might well be given up for lost. The relief ship might turn back without him, her captain anxious to avoid the risk of being hemmed in by pack-ice. He had, after all, to consider the greatest good of the greatest number, rather than just one man, even though he was the leader of the expedition. Mawson knew that there was the ever-present danger of a build-up of ice-floes along that stretch of Antarctic coastline known as the Shackleton Ice Shelf.

A morning came at last when Mawson knew that he must weigh up the chances positively, and come to a decision. So near, and yet so far, was the phrase that rang in his head as he pondered his problem. Then, snapping his fingers at Fate, he made up his mind. For better or for worse, he would leave Aladdin's Cave and tackle those last few miles. Better to die—if die he must—on his feet, battling with the elements, than fade away in the ice cave. The change of diet had done one thing for him, at least—the fruit seemed to have cured the stomach pains with which he had been racked for so many weeks past. True, his feet were agonizingly painful, but he could do nothing about this until he reached base and had access to a well-equipped medicine chest. He picked up the ropes of his sled once more, said a grateful farewell to Aladdin's Cave, and set out bravely into the blizzard.

And now his luck changed, taking a turn for the better. Within an hour of his leaving the cave, the blizzard began to ease. Soon, though the wind still blew, there was no more than a sprinkling of snow with it. As the air cleared, he could see, near the water's edge, the huts erected when Main Base was established. Inside it, he had no doubt, the other members of the party would be huddled around the stove, speculating as to where their leader might be. Probably, now that the blizzard had eased, they would be preparing to mount another search-party. They had too much sense to set out in search of anyone in conditions such as had prevailed for the last week and more. In such conditions, they well knew, two parties could pass within yards of one another and be totally unaware of each other's existence.

Then, suddenly, he was brought up short in his tracks. The relief ship *Aurora*—where was she? According to the note he had found in the cairn, she was at anchor in Commonwealth Bay. But if so—where was she anchored? Though the air was now clear, he could see no sign of her at all. His heart sank. He recalled that a date had been set on which Captain Davis was to take his ship along the ice shelf to carry supplies to a party of explorers many miles to the west. That date, then, must have come—and gone!

For a moment or two something like final despair seized Douglas Mawson. He had left the ice cave with the words "So near and yet so far" chiming in his head. Now those words had taken on a new and wholly sinister meaning. But, he told himself, there was nothing he could do about this development. All he could do was to press on, and continue to hope. So, once more he picked up his sled ropes and began to march on toward the base.

His faith and determination were rewarded, and in twofold fashion. As he approached Main Base, with perhaps only two or three miles still to cover, he spotted *Aurora* lying out in the bay. She had been hidden from him until then by the great mass of Cape Denison. True, she was steaming westward, as had been agreed between himself and her captain many months before. But there was a radio set at Main Base, so she could easily be recalled before she was out of range.

And at that moment he was spotted from the hut. At once a swarm of men emerged, waving wildly and beginning to race and stumble up the long ice slope in his direction. One of them turned back almost at once, and Mawson knew instinctively that he had gone to the hut to radio Captain Davis.

He was right. By the time he reached Main Base, accompanied now by every other member of the Expedition, riding in style on his own broken sled hauled by his companions in triumph, he could see that *Aurora* had begun to make a wide sweep across the bay, bound again for the anchorage she had so recently left.

Douglas Mawson's terrible ordeal was over at last. He had been away from Main Base for some three months, during which he had been continuously on the march. He had lost first one and then the other of his companions on the trek. He had covered the last hundred miles and more solo, dragging a mutilated sled. When he had to take shelter, all his resources had been a tattered sheet of canvas rigged on a pair of skis. He had subsisted on starvation rations for weeks on end, kept alive only by his indomitable spirit, a fanatical determination to see this thing through to the bitter end.

The five parties that had been given specific tasks to carry out during Mawson's absence all succeeded in fulfilling them, but it should be remembered that their challenge was in no way comparable with that undertaken by their leader, which so very nearly cost him his life and did cost the lives of his two companions.

It took him some time to recover his health and strength after his miraculous return to Main Base, where his companions lovingly and admiringly cared for him. Much work remained to be done. Some of it had been envisaged from the start, while other work was the result of what had confronted the men on their arrival. Soundings had to be taken, wind velocities and pressures had to be estimated and recorded, as did the fluctuating temperatures—some of which reached figures hard to believe unless they were actually experienced. The radio receiver and transmitter, which was an improvised affair and for a long time proved wholly ineffectual, had to be properly installed, improved in performance, and maintained.

Not until February, 1914, was the small party finally taken aboard *Aurora,* to sail for home, the main objectives of the Australasian Antarctic Expedition gloriously fulfilled —though two fine men had tragically lost their lives. Later that year, in June, Douglas Mawson was summoned to Buckingham Palace, there to be knighted by King George V for his magnificent courage and the splendor of his achievement. Few explorers, whether in Antarctica or elsewhere, can ever have deserved the honor more.

Wilfred P. Thesiger in the Empty Quarter

Wilfred Thesiger is one of the great lone travelers of this century. His dominant interest has always been in pioneer journeys through little-known territories, especially in Africa and the Middle East. One region that particularly attracted him is the Arabian Desert, over half a million square miles in extent—more than four times the total area of the British Isles. It is hardly known to Europeans, though Bertram Thomas and St. John Philby have explored some parts of it. So desolate is the central portion of this vast desert, which lies between the Persian Gulf and the Gulf of Oman to the east, and the Red Sea to the west, that it is known as the Empty Quarter. It comprises roughly half of the Arabian Desert, or 250,000 square miles in all. To the Arab tribes, notably the one known as the Rashids, who roam in these inhospitable parts, it is known simply as "The Sands."

In 1946 Thesiger was commissioned by the British Government to explore as much as possible of the region with the objective of locating the centers where the locusts breed and multiply. The Middle East Anti-Locust Unit was anxious if possible to stamp out this traditional and terrible pest, for in their annual migrations the vast swarms could completely devastate all crops and vegetation throughout wide areas and bring starvation and death to those who depended on them for bare survival. The commission was a most welcome one, for Thesiger realized that it would call upon all the powers of endurance, resourcefulness and cour-

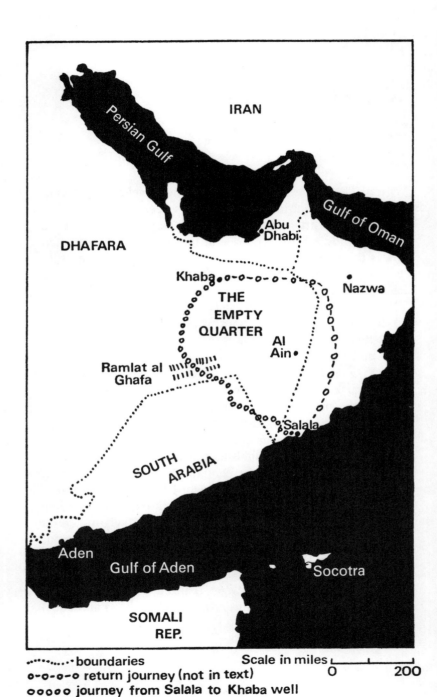

age he possessed. The area, too, was one which he had long been anxious to explore in depth.

Thesiger enlisted the services of a number of Bedouin tribesmen, all of whom professed to know the Sands well. Late in October, with this escort and an ample camel train, he set off northward from Salala, on the south coast of Arabia, heading for the Empty Quarter. Anticipating that he would be away from his base at least two months, he made sure before he set out that he was well equipped. He had loaded onto his camels a large supply of flour, some four hundred pounds of rice, maize, dried fish, sugar, coffee, tea, butter and other items. Ample supplies of water were carried, in the Bedouin tradition, in goatskins. For meat, they would rely on what they could shoot down. As a former army officer, Thesiger knew exactly what he required in the way of weapons. He had a long-barreled .303 Martini rifle, and also a lighter .303 sporting model—and he had ample ammunition for both guns.

After a few days on the march, as they were approaching the southern fringe of the Empty Quarter, a number of his Bedouin companions, for no clear reason at all, announced that they would go no farther. Thesiger tried to find out the reason for this unexpected betrayal of their promise, but without success. He argued with them but they were obstinate—as only Bedouins can be obstinate. With some reluctance, he divided the store of provisions so that at least the men would have enough food and water to keep them going after they turned back. They were unreasonably demanding about this, and he knew quite well that their intention was to secure as large a quantity as possible so that they could share what they had with their families on their return. So, they parted—the defaulting tribesmen southward to rejoin their fellows, the faithful Rashid tribesmen northward with their leader.

Thesiger was none too happy about the inroads that had

been made into his store of provisions. A great quantity of food seemed to have been spirited away. He knew the tradition of the desert—that you never refused food or drink to anyone you chanced to meet, whether known to you or otherwise. His stores had to suffice not only his depleted party, but chance-met desert rangers during the many weeks to follow. He had already had experience of this, when his escort had given lavishly of their stores to groups of camel-borne tribesmen they had encountered. It had seemed to him on those occasions that his men felt a greater loyalty to the other Bedouin than they felt toward him—the man who employed them and was paying them their wages!

With al Auf, his chief guide and right-hand man, he examined the position seriously. In all, they calculated that there now remained to them about two hundred pounds of flour, a few bags of rice, a little maize, and some butter, sugar and tea. Al Auf assured him, however, that they would come to a splendid oasis, or rather an area of oases known as the Liwa. There, he said, they would find food, and all the water they coud possibly require, both for themselves and for their camels. He was asked how far it was to Liwa. The answer was not an encouraging one—a month of hard marching, he was told. Perhaps longer than that.

Thesiger did some rapid calculation. His party numbered only twelve now, but their supplies had fallen so low that each man's daily ration could be no more than half a pound of either flour or maize. The other vital commodity was of course water. He estimated that they now had barely enough to give each man one quart per day—not enough to quench his thirst, let alone serve for cooking or washing. And this calculation was based on the assumption that they would reach the first oasis, or at least some trickle of stagnant water, within three weeks at the most.

Al Auf had said it would be a month before they reached the oasis. He reminded Thesiger that three weeks was the maximum period during which a camel could carry its load across a desert without replenishment of its own water supply, and even this was possible only if the camel came across sufficient grazing of the right kind. Thesiger knew well that the problem of maintaining the strength of their camels was a vital one. If their transport failed, then they were lost men, doomed to die in the desert.

Would they come across any good grazing, al Auf was asked. The Rashid tribesman answered with conviction. He knew the Sands well, and there would be good grazing at least as far as the point on the map shown as Ramlat al Ghafa, for it was known that rain had fallen there as recently as two years ago—a better record than could be quoted for many other parts of the region.

He was proved right. There was grazing at their next camp, the first one they established after the breakaway group had departed southward. And while the camels grazed, a gazelle was spotted and shot. The party ate half of it for their supper, then secreted the remainder in a thorn bush so that they could start off the next day with a good breakfast. But next morning, to their great disappointment, it had vanished. One of the Bedouin recognized the spoor of a desert fox, undoubtedly the thief-in-the-night. Following its spoor, they came to the point where the fox had buried the half-carcass, of which it had eaten only a little. They beat the sand off it and brought it back to the camp in triumph. So, breakfast was a good meal after all, and they could set off in good heart.

Now they were entering the true Empty Quarter. Ghanim was their next objective, but the march was to prove hard going indeed. The terrain alternated between near-level stretches and enormous sand dunes, some of them two and even three hundred feet in height. Sometimes they could be skirted. Just as often they had to be surmounted, and the effort of doing this was more and more exhausting. One face or other, according to the direction of the wind that had formed the dune, would be almost impossibly steep. The other would be less steep, but composed of particles of sand so loose that marching over them was like struggling over quicksand tilted on its side.

Beyond Ghanim they came at length to a site which, al Auf said, might prove to contain water. It bore the name of a Bedouin, Kaur bin Atarit, who had discovered it when he and his beasts were dying of thirst. It is true, there was a sort of well there, though it was in fact little more than a depression in the hard gypsum floor that extended in all directions, immediately beneath a thin layer of coarse sand. The men scratched and scraped at it with bowls and other utensils in the hope of finding drinkable water at the bottom. At the end of two hours' hard work, there was a glint of moisture to reward them, and they redoubled their frantic efforts. Now they were rewarded with a smear of water filled with grit. The men drank it as best they could, and smacked their lips over it. Thesiger found it as foul as any water he had ever tasted. During the night, the water accumulated, and before they left for the next day's march they had filled one of the goatskins, filtering away as much of the sand as possible from the water as they did so.

During the next few days they ate one meal only between striking camp and making their next camp, between dawn and dusk. It was not an appetizing meal. A curious sort of porridge made of their foul water and a mixture of flour and maize. In between they gnawed at gritty lumps of unleavened bread, smeared with a thin covering of rancid butter. This of course only served to intensify their thirst. The temptation to drink deeply from their goatskins was fierce, and continuous, but all of them knew that to preserve their water was absolutely vital, and they must ration themselves strictly because of the ever-present risk of reaching an oasis that would turn out to be bone dry. This was every desert traveler's permanent nightmare.

Camp sites offered problems, too. Not the least of these was the presence of the large, pale-green desert scorpions.

The horned viper was another pest. Though it would not deliberately attack a human being, the viper would eject its fierce poison into any foot that was unlucky enough to tread on it in the dark. Curiously enough, though Thesiger had little fear of scorpions or of horned vipers, he had, for another creature, a loathing so intense that he hardly understood it himself. The creature in question was the desert spider. He knew perfectly well that the desert spider was absolutely harmless, but they *looked* evil. Their bodies were as broad as the palm of a man's hand, and loathsomely potbellied. They had long, hairy legs, reddish in hue and frantically nimble. All in all, they were, Thesiger unreasonably felt, hateful creatures. For all his experience of deserts, both in Arabia and in the Kalahari itself, he never came to terms with them.

The going became progressively harder. Water was an unceasing, ever-menacing problem. They came to a waterhole that at first promised well. But the supply of water it contained proved to be so foul that even the camels, who were desperately thirsty, refused to drink. Knowing that their own lives depended on the ability of the camels to keep going, the Bedouin tried to force them to drink by blocking their nostrils, but they struggled so violently that more drastic measures had to be taken. The camel men threw the beasts to the ground, and while two men tilted their heads, a third forced water between their gaping jaws. It was not a pleasant sight, and the camels fought back strenuously.

One morning, at the very end of November, Thesiger woke to find his men in conference. There was obviously a strong difference of opinion among them. His trusty guide, al Auf, was gesticulating violently. Thesiger thought it wise to remain aloof. All in good time, no doubt, he would learn what the trouble was. And, as he anticipated, he learned it from al Auf. A number of the Bedouin, he was told, had decided to take their share of what food remained to them and turn back along the trail. They were convinced, it seemed, that to venture farther into the Sands would mean certain death for themselves and for their camels.

Once again the provisions were divided. Thesiger now had only four Bedouin still faithful to him. They retained fifty pounds of flour and maize, some coffee, a little of the long-rancid butter, some sugar and tea and some dried onions. They insisted on retaining four of the strongest camels, and bought from the other men a fifth camel. It was a poor beast, but could, in a desperate emergency, be killed for food, though this was a thought that Thesiger put out of his mind in abhorrence.

So, once again, a sorely diminished party set off northward into the dead heart of the Empty Quarter: Wilfred Thesiger, his right-hand man al Auf, and three other Rashid tribesmen, bin Kabina, Mabkhaut and Musallim. Strangely enough, the four Bedouin now seemed more cheerful than they had been for many days past. Thesiger suspected one reason for this—the men knew that they had taken up a challenge, and had remained loyal to their leader where their fellow tribesmen had betrayed him. There was another, more obvious reason. He had promised that at the end of their desert journey he would present his guns to them as gifts. To any Bedouin, a gun is his most precious possession. Al Auf and his fellows knew that the guns they would receive were infinitely superior to those owned by the other Bedouin with whom they had contact, friendly or otherwise.

Their daily ration of water was now down to a bare pint per man. But they had their first stroke of luck soon after they set out when they encountered a group of tribesmen who were closely related to the Rashid and at once recognized al Auf. They were camped at a spot where, admittedly, there was no water supply, but there was a patch of excellent grazing. They had thirty-five camels with them, all in first-class condition. It was here that Thesiger was to witness, for the first time in the Arabian Desert, that hospitality which is traditional among even the most independent Bedouin tribes. His party was bidden to halt and join them. Bowls of camel milk—a rare delicacy after the foul and brackish water that had been their sole liquid refreshment for so many days past—were set before them.

He watched one of the camels being milked. A young Bedouin boy approached the camel, talked to her soothingly, stroked her udder, making it plain to her what she must do. Then, when he could tell that she was ready to let down her milk, he raised his right leg until he could rest his foot on his left knee, standing steadily on one thin brown leg. With accustomed hands he pulled and squeezed the teats, and soon his bowl held as much as two quarts of rich milk, frothing like good soapy lather. The Bedouin to whom he handed it blew the froth off into the air and then drank deeply from what lay beneath it, smacking his thin lips in contentment after each long drink.

There was milk to spare among those generous Bedouin, for a number of their camels were "in milk," and they were staying on at that camp site to fatten their beasts before traveling farther into the Sands. Al Auf filled the party's goatskins with milk, saying to Thesiger that they would be able later to mix it with any water they came across. However foul it might be, the milk would make it more drinkable. Thesiger reflected grimly as to what the milk would be like after being carried in a goatskin already impregnated with foul water, on a camel's back, over burning sands, perhaps for many days on end. But he knew better than to utter his thoughts out loud. This was generosity, and he must be grateful for it. In fact, they kept that milk for more than a week. It turned sour, of course, acquiring a taste something like yoghurt, but mixed with the equally sour water, it did in fact prove curiously refreshing. Al Auf told him that this was a regular practice among the Bedouin and that they actually had a name for this mixture of brackish water and sour camel milk—they called it "shanin."

They left the camp early in the morning in the hope that they might cover a fair distance across the desert before the sun rose to its zenith and made every movement an agony. As always, the sand, in spite of the heat it had absorbed during the previous day, was bitterly cold. The men walked instead of riding their camels, in an attempt to keep the blood circulating in their veins and work the stiffness out of their joints caused by sleeping on thin rugs on the open sand during the night. By now all of them, Thesiger included, had deep fissures in the soles and heels of their feet, the direct result of alternating extreme heat and extreme cold. Sand penetrated these cracks and was pressed farther and farther into them as they walked.

Alternately walking alongside their camels and riding them, they traveled throughout that long day. The desert was more arid than any part they had met with so far. Sand dunes rose to nearly five hundred feet. Skirting them involved slithering sideways and using up energy of which they had little enough to spare simply to preserve their equilibrium. One of the camels, which happened to be carrying their two largest goatskins, tripped and fell. From behind, Thesiger could see what was happening, and prayed that it would fall in such a way as not to burst the precious goatskins. His silent prayer was answered. Musallim managed to get the camel to its feet, though it was kicking out frantically in all directions, as only a camel can kick. Mercifully neither of the goatskins had suffered, an enormous relief to them all.

That evening the wind rose, and they made haste to camp while it was still possible to erect some sort of shelter. The camels were hobbled, and al Auf set about preparing the first drink any of them would have had all day. The

Bedouin were given a pint each of water mixed with a little sour milk. Thesiger himself preferred to take his ration of water, which smelt unbearably foul as it was squeezed out of the goatskin, and made it a little less unpalatable by mixing with it some crushed cinnamon, some ginger and a few cloves. This might seem a strange mixture of ingredients, but they would at least do something to disguise the appalling taste.

While al Auf measured out the water and milk, Musallim set about preparing a meal. It could hardly have been simpler or less appetizing. He carefully measured out each man's ration of flour—about three pounds in all for the five of them—and proceeded to bake a sort of unleavened, doughy bread. They sat around the fire and each man took his share, dipped it into some melted butter at the bottom of a pan, and then, muttering "In the name of Allah," ate. Afterwards bin Kabina gave them each a mouthful or so of rank coffee. It was their one meal of the day, and very soon after it was finished, having made sure that their camels were securely hobbled, they lay down beneath the stars and fell into the sleep of exhaustion.

Next day they came to an area of sand dunes so enormous that all the ones they had encountered until then seemed in comparison to have been mere molehills. Thesiger estimated that one of them must have been between six and seven hundred feet high. Contrasted with the endless stretches of near-level gypsum over which they had been marching for some time past, it seemed like a mountain, a mountain of coarse red sand. It took them more than an hour to skirt its vast bulk and regain the direction they should be following. On the north side of it they entered a region of salt flats, burning white and painfully dazzling to the eyes. Thesiger looked back, shading his eyes against the glare. It seemed to his feverish imagination that the monster sand dune stood there, blocking the track behind them to the south, menacing them with the message that they were now indeed prisoners of the Empty Quarter.

The problem of water was constantly with them. One thing that worried them was the fact that some of the goatskins seemed to be leaking. Al Auf located the small holes and plugged them with thorns from the occasional camel-thorn bushes they encountered alongside their track. But the continuous jolting the goatskins were forced to endure soon resulted in more leaks, not always immediately detected. It was agonizing to see a trickle of the precious fluid running down the camel's side, and not to know how long this had been going on. Because of this incessant anxiety about water they had to keep on the move far longer than would ordinarily have been reckoned a day's march.

One day they stopped for a scanty meal at sundown. The sense of desolation was more acute than ever. Thesiger, with his four Bedouin companions, felt that he was in a lost world. Or rather, that they were in a tiny self-contained world of their own, utterly isolated from the whole of the great world beyond the desert. Al Auf had recently told him that he had once made this same journey, some years before, without other companions. "Quite alone, were you?" Thesiger asked him. And the Bedouin had turned on him a look of genuine puzzlement. "No," he had replied soberly, "I had God for my companion, so I was not alone."

After the meal they started off again, and rode for two long hours across a salt flat. They did not customarily ride, or walk, by night, but the shortage of water had made this necessary. In the strong, clear moonlight the sand dunes seemed larger than they really were. The shapes they assumed, with the dark shadows cast across them by their undulating crests, were strange, even sinister. The air temperature dropped dramatically as soon as the sun had vanished beneath the horizon. Thesiger found himself shivering uncontrollably. The cold crept up his limbs and invaded his whole being. He dismounted from his camel in the hope of staving off complete collapse by keeping on the move, but his legs did not seem to belong to him any more. The pain caused by the sand wedged into the cracks in his soles and heels was almost more than he could bear without crying out aloud. He was glad that his four faithful companions had now broken into song, and he listened to them enviously.

At last they were too exhausted, men and beasts alike, to go a step farther, and they finally halted to make the best they could of what was left of the night. Thesiger would have given all he possessed for the chance of a long, hot drink, but he knew that with the scanty resources left to them he would have to wait many hours before he next had a drink. The men lit a fire to warm themselves, and all of them lay down and tried to sleep. But sleep was slow to come, for him at any rate, for he was chilled to the bone and utterly exhausted by the day's march. When he did at length fall asleep he dreamed continuously of cool, clear, sweet running water. Each time he woke he felt colder than before. For all his dreams, it was a nightmare of a night.

At first hint of light his companions were up and about, to make the earliest possible start and cover as much ground as they could before the worst heat of the day. There were still endless miles of salt flats to be crossed. They consisted of crusts of coarse salt so sharp that they cut their feet. The air was still so cold, for the sun was not yet up, that Thesiger's eyes stung and watered. The water that ran down his cheeks into the corners of his mouth was salt and brackish to the taste. He wondered whether perhaps al Auf, marching by his side, thought he was weeping from pain and cold.

As the light improved they could see ahead of them what appeared to be a range of high hills, if not actually mountains. In desert conditions it is difficult to judge with any degree of accuracy either distances or heights. They might not be mountains, or even hills, but by contrast with the near-level salt flats over which they had been plodding they looked to be something more than dunes.

After some hours of marching they came within range of them. They were indeed sand dunes, but absolute monsters. They were not isolated dunes that could be bypassed, but a range of dunes—rounded summits alternating with saddlelike passes. Thesiger estimated that even the passes must be seven or eight hundred feet above the level of the salt flats, and these had, somehow, to be surmounted if the little party were not to be forced to turn back in its tracks, defeated. He noted that this time the steep side was the one facing them. It was a daunting prospect.

Al Auf announced that he would go off and reconnoiter. There was, he felt sure, a route that they could successfully take. He handed his camel's headrope to Mabkhaut, and set off on foot, carrying a rifle with him in the hope of shooting something for the cooking pot. The rest of the party watched him walking away toward the foothills, and shook their heads. "He will have to find a way around," one said to the other. "None of our camels could cross this range." They seemed resigned to their fate, and Thesiger was reminded yet again of the fundamental difference, in these matters, between West and East, between Christian and Muslim.

He left his companions and went and sat down by himself. Strangely, the salt flat beneath him was icy cold, though the air about him was already shimmering with the heat from the sun now soaring to its zenith. He looked at the enormous barrier of sand confronting them, the barrier that somehow they simply had to conquer. It was astonishing that so huge a rampart could have been built there simply by the force of the wind blowing across the desert. He could see the tiny, purposeful figure of al Auf plodding forward, his beloved rifle on his shoulder, in search of a track that they might be able to tackle successfully. He was now ascending a steep ridge, and looked like some mountaineer tackling an *arête* on some formidable mountain expedition.

What, he asked himself, were they to do, if al Auf returned with the news that there simply was no practicable route to the saddle between those peaks? One possibility was to unload the camels' burdens and carry them over the top on their own backs, making perhaps a dozen laborious journeys up and back again, and then finally leading the camels by their headropes, freed from their loads, assisting them to make the crossing. It was not an inviting prospect. It would entail an almost superhuman physical effort, and they would not be able to refresh themselves while undertaking it, for they had so scanty a supply of water remaining to them.

Even if they did succeed in crossing this formidable obstacle, who knew but that there might be another similar, or worse rampart only a day's march beyond? And another beyond that, and yet another beyond that? Angrily, Thesiger rebuked himself for entertaining such craven fears. This was no mood in which to undertake and see through this project to which he had so enthusiastically committed himself! Besides—what would those other Bedouin, the defaulters, say when they learned that he too had turned back, defeated? He braced himself and told himself sternly that, come what might, he would accomplish this objective.

After a while he saw al Auf returning. He was walking with a vigorous step. The four men watched his approach, and kept silent. Al Auf went to his camel, picked up the headrope, and spoke one word. "Come," he said.

The rest of the party fell into line behind him. Al Auf led them to an incline that seemed less steep, when they came near it, than it had from afar. This was perhaps due in part to the angle at which a shadow lay across it. It proved to be the first of a succession of sloping terraces of loose sand that seemed to rise like huge slanting steps most of the way to the saddle between the two main summits. The sand was soft, and as soon as they set their feet on it it collapsed beneath their weight, continuously shifting in a sinister fashion, like dry quicksands. From his reading, Thesiger knew that such areas of quicksand were to be encountered, always without warning, in any desert. But he had implicit faith in his trusty guide, al Auf, as had the other men, and al Auf was now marching ahead without hesitation, up the slope.

They followed, in single file. Al Auf led them diagonally across each inclined terrace in turn until he reached a ridge of harder, firmer sand that lay along its upper edge. There he turned back again, to cross the next terrace in another diagonal line, his feet and his camel's hoofs sinking deep into the loose sand, until once again the loose sand gave place to the firmer sand that composed the ridge on the farther side. Thesiger was filled with admiration. As so often before, this Rashid tribesman, al Auf, was proving that he was a true native of the Sands and knew their ways to the last detail, as a river pilot knows the sandbanks and currents over which he must take a ship.

The camels struggled. But for the herculean efforts of their drivers they would have lain down and refused to go farther. From time to time one of them did so, but his driver had means of getting it on its feet again. After a brief, strenuous halt the party would push on again, up and ever up toward that longed-for saddle between the summits.

At last they reached the saddle, and threw themselves down onto the burning sand completely exhausted. After they had rested for a short time, al Auf gave the signal to start off again. Thesiger meanwhile had been studying the terrain to the north of this saddle in the huge sand dune. He saw before him a rolling expanse of smooth-looking sand interspersed with occasional dunes, but none of them, so far as he could guess, of the same scale as the one they had just climbed. There were also what appeared from this distance to be shallow valleys. This encouraged him to hope that there might be water to be found among them. But in any case there should be better browsing for their camels than any they had found for some time past. So long as their beasts of burden were reasonably fit, there was hope for them all. "Come," said al Auf, and they began the long descent of the northern face of the giant dune.

It proved easier by far than the ascent of the south face had been. Nevertheless they took the precaution of holding their beasts by their headropes to steady them on the alternating slopes and hollows. The north face of the mountain-like sand dune consisted of an infinite number of small, irregularly shaped dunes, separated from one another by channels. Sometimes the sand was firm underfoot, at other times they sank deep into it and had to make an enormous effort to prevent themselves from being dragged forward by the clumsy weight of their camels and running the risk of breaking their legs before they could extricate them from the tenacious grip of the sand.

But at last they had descended the foothills and were on near-level terrain once more. There was a stretch of those bitter salt flats to cross, to begin with, but after the ascent and descent of that sand barrier this was almost easy going. They would have to march well into the night to make up for the time lost in surmounting this rampart of wind-blown sand that now rose behind them.

As they rode on, Thesiger found himself becoming overwhelmed with a great desire, an imperative need, in fact, to sleep. Even the ungainly motion of the camel he was riding was not sufficient to keep him properly awake. He made desperate efforts to keep awake, in the full knowledge that if he did not do so he might well fall from the perch on his camel's back and receive an injury that might make the difference between failure and success—if nothing worse than that.

They rode in complete silence for four interminable hours that afternoon before coming to a halt in order to rest the camels. One of the camels, the poorest of them, immediately lay down. This is always a bad sign, evidence of exhaustion so great that the animal is not prepared to go in search of sustenance, however badly it is in need at the time. Not that it would have found such sustenance, even if it had gone in search of it. Once more, the terrain was salt flat, nothing but salt flat. The promise held out to the men as they had looked down on it from the summit had not been fulfilled. It was a bitter disappointment for them all.

At sunset they made yet another start, though neither men nor camels were refreshed. They marched on until midnight, when al Auf called a halt for the second time that day. "We must have some rest," he said. "Tomorrow we have to cross Uruq al Shaiba."

The announcement came as a shock to Thesiger. He knew of Uruq al Shaiba by repute—a monster rampart of sand that had to be crossed somewhere on the way between Ramlat al Ghafa, which he knew they had long since passed, and Sabhaka. But he had been telling himself that this great barrier that they had been fighting their way across *was* Uruq al Shaiba, though al Auf had not in fact spoken of it by name.

He put the point to his guide. Al Auf looked at him with a curious smile on his swarthy face. "It was only a dune that we crossed today," he said quietly. "We shall come to Uruq al Shaiba in the heat of tomorrow's sun. So, now we should sleep." When Thesiger did eventually fall asleep, it was to dream, not of streams of clear, cool, sweet water but of a sand dune rising into the heavens until it dwarfed the highest mountains in the world.

He was wakened before it was yet light by the shouts of al Auf and his companions rounding up the camels. Bin Kabina brewed a small container of coffee and they drank a few drops of it each. All too soon the last had vanished down their throats—hardly enough to warm them in the bitter cold of early morning. There were still stars in the sky, and there was only the barest hint of dawn far away on the eastern horizon.

They warmed themselves as best they could by the embers of the fire they had lit at midnight when they broke off their long day's march. Then, with a brief "Come," al Auf strode off, stamping in the loose sand to get the circulation going again in his feet, though the deep cracks in the skin and flesh, hardened by the cold, made him wince as he did so. The sand was like fragmented particles of ice to the touch. In a few hours' time it would be burning hot, as though it were embers beneath their feet.

They came in due course in sight of a range of sand dunes that made even the giant of the previous day seem insignificant. Al Auf pointed ahead, and spoke its name: Uruq al Shaiba. This range had sharply pointed peaks, instead of the rounded domes that had characterized the earlier one. It looked as though there must be rock as well as sand up there, though Thesiger knew that this could not in fact be so. But at least the formation in general suggested that the sand might be firmer, less easily dislodged as they climbed over it. And there were saddles between each peak and its neighbor. It was for the least high of these that al Auf was now making. Thesiger reminded himself that his guide had traveled this way before. The thought of confronting, challenging and mastering such obstacles with no human companion beside him to encourage him made him hold his breath in wonder. What al Auf had done alone, he reflected, surely they, as a close-knit party, could and would achieve.

Contrary to his hopes, at least among the foothills of this great range of dunes, the sand was as soft and treacherous as any they had encountered. Very soon, in spite of the great spongy cushions of their hoofs, the camels were in difficulty. They floundered more and more dangerously, and when every so often they were brought to a halt by an apparently insurmountable ridge of shifting sand, their great legs trembled violently and they moaned aloud, a piteous, discordant roaring sound that was heart-rending, even frightening to listen to.

From time to time one or other of them simply lay down and gave every appearance of having resolved never to rise again. There was only one thing to do—unload what it was carrying and set to work to get it on its feet again through a mixture of coaxing and sheer muscular force. It was a never-ending task, strenuous, frustrating and often seeming to be quite hopeless. The sun had risen high overhead while they were still only part way up the main slope. Wrestling with refractory camels, Thesiger, who was himself almost at his last gasp from continuous and unassuaged thirst, felt dizziness invading his whole being. His heart thumped wildly in his rib cage, his ears sang, his muscles seemed to have turned to water. He felt drained of everything. He retched continually, and believed he would have been sick time and time again if there had been anything in his stomach. In such conditions, sunstroke seemed almost certain.

There was continuous shouting from the camel men, to match the squeals and roaring of the beasts as they struggled up that never-ending slope of shifting, treacherous sand. One after another they fell, were unloaded, manhandled to their feet once more and reloaded, to stagger upward for another few hundred yards before collapsing once again. More than once Thesiger himself fell to the sand, which was now scorching hot, rested his weary limbs for a moment or two, and then struggled to his feet yet again. He wondered how often he could repeat the exercise before falling down, never to rise again. But sheer pride made him fight on, rather than permit his Bedouin companions to see how near to the end of his tether he had come.

It took them three hours of toil and sweat and agony to reach the top of Uruq al Shaiba. There they rested. When he had recovered his breath and his heartbeats had returned to something like normal, Thesiger looked out ahead of where they were lying, to ascertain what sort of going now lay ahead of them. It was not an encouraging sight. Instead of the gently undulating terrain onto which they had passed when they had descended from the previous sand barrier there now seemed to be a succession of lesser dunes, each one of which would have to be negotiated by men and beasts already exhausted by the struggles of the last few hours.

These smaller dunes, it is true, merged into a region of salt flats, but immediately beyond these there appeared to be yet another complex of sand dunes, each higher and more forbidding than the last. Some of them could quite possibly be as high as the one on which they were now standing, though al Auf assured him that this was not so. "Uruq al Shaiba we have passed. It is the worst," he said, and he spoke with conviction.

It might have been the worst, but what lay immediately ahead looked bad enough. From this height, Thesiger could see to a far distant horizon. In that enormous expanse of sand and salt flat he could see no living thing, whether animal or scanty shrub or lowly camel-thorn. It was a lunar landscape—but pitilessly hot. And it had to be crossed—for there was to be no going back now. A sort of despair, which he recognized but found himself unable to check, overwhelmed him. "There is nowhere to go," he muttered to himself. "We can't go back, and certainly our poor camels will never be able to tackle any more sand dunes like this. This, surely, looks like the end for us all."

Somehow, though, they managed to descend the succession of small dunes to the salt flats at their foot. They worked their way down a shallow valley beyond them, and, with considerably greater effort, up the further side. There they were forced by sheer exhaustion to break their custom and halt, even though it was still only midday. Al Auf distributed enough water for each man to wet his lips and tongue. There was not sufficient for them to have a real drink, or even to swallow a little sip.

They rested there for two hours or less. Perhaps "rest" is not the right word, for the sand was so hot beneath them that it was impossible to stay long in any one position. At the end of two hours they set off again, determined to march at least until sundown to make up for the time they had spent laboriously crossing the great sand range, the notorious Uruq al Shaiba. With every hour's marching, though, they were that much nearer to the promise of water. Al Auf pointed to the great sand dunes that rose into the blue sky ahead of them and told Thesiger that though it was impossible to see, from where they now were, any route past or through these, in fact there was such a route, and he knew it. It was a route he had found for himself on his previous journey, and he would guide them safely along it.

For a while the going was a little easier. The intervening dunes, instead of lying across their route, now lay to one side or the other. So they marched between these ramparts of sand instead of having continuously to ascend and descend them. But Al Auf was setting a hard pace. It was essential, he urged, that they must make their best possible speed over the easier terrain if they were to reach a waterhole before the last few drops remaining to them vanished.

They came to a stretch of course vegetation, and stopped immediately to allow the camels to graze. They went frantic in their efforts to snatch at what was available to them. The sun was setting and it was quite dark when they moved on. They could continue their march in the cool of the evening. Then, as on the previous night, they would halt, light a fire, eat a scanty meal, snatch a few hours of broken sleep, and set off again at first hint of light. So they marched on until midnight when once again sheer exhaustion brought them to a halt. They were on the march again the next morning before dawn had broken.

They marched for four hours without a break, intent on making the best speed they could while the terrain was relatively easy beneath their feet and before the sun had become unbearably hot. There were dunes to surmount, but none of them, difficult as they were, were comparable with those they had already encountered and conquered. They came to a cluster of scrub bushes and startled a desert hare from its lowly cover. Quick as a flash al Auf struck it to the ground with a stick, and bin Kabina cried out in joy, "God has given us meat!"

The temptation to halt there and then, light a fire and cook the hare was great, but it had to be resisted. For the remainder of the day's march the five men thought of nothing but the meal they would enjoy that evening when at last they felt able to make camp. For many days past they had subsisted on small quantities of Musallim's unleavened bread, smeared with a little rancid butter that left a taste in the mouth which Thesiger, at least, found utterly revolting. For days past their empty stomachs had rumbled, with nothing in them that really appeased their ever-increasing hunger. Now, with the prospect of a change of diet, if only for one small meal, they marched on cheerfully, licking their cracked lips in anticipation.

By mutual consent they halted that day before sundown. Mabkhaut gathered fuel, including the precious camel dung which is used as such by all nomadic tribes, and lit a fire. There was some argument as to how the hare should be cooked. Mabkhaut was for roasting it in its skin in the embers. By that method, he pointed out, they would not need to use any of their precious water to cook it. Bin Kabina would not hear of this. Charred meat, such as would result from Mabkhaut's method, would be dry and hard to swallow. What they really needed was a good meat soup, even if this meant using a little more of their precious water.

God had sent them meat—it would be insulting if they did not turn it to the best possible use! It was a good argument, and with it bin Kabina won the day.

Or rather, a compromise was reached. The hare was cooked in a more orthodox fashion and the greater part of it was carefully divided into five equal portions. Each portion was pitifully small, for the Arabian desert hare is not very large even when full-grown, and this one was in fact only part grown. However, it was meat—a commodity they had begun to believe they would never see or taste again. Then, to make sure that no man was treated unfairly, the five portions were named as lots and a number of tallies were prepared. These were shuffled, and then each man drew his portion according to the tally he held in his hand.

Suddenly there was an exclamation from bin Kabina. He had omitted to include the diminutive hare's liver! One and all of them, the four Bedouin declared that their leader, Umbarak, as they called him, must have this extra, this delicacy. Thesiger did his utmost to decline, and persuade them to draw lots for it, but the men were adamant in their refusal to benefit from bin Kabina's oversight. In the end Thesiger accepted, believing that otherwise he might offend his generous companions.

As al Auf had promised, the going did become progressively easier once the sand dunes were passed. There were stretches of salt flats, there were sand dunes, there were areas where a little camel-scrub grew and their beasts could browse and recoup their strength. But there was still no sign of water. And there was only enough flour left to make loaves that would provide a few mouthfuls per man per day for a week.

But now they were approaching the edge of the Dhafara district of the Sands and al Auf was certain that they would come upon water within three days at most if they could maintain their present pace. There was a well which he knew by name—Khaba. Thesiger asked him if he knew of any possibility of water before that well was reached and al Auf answered that he knew of a small waterhole about halfway to Khaba, but he could not promise that it would contain water. And anyway, last time he was there the water was so foul that his camel could not be persuaded, even by force, to drink. This time, however, he said, there were sufficient men to force their camels to drink, and this they must certainly do when the chance came, for they were at the end of their resources.

They set off early in the morning and marched for seven hours without a halt. At midday, exhausted by the heat and lack of food and water, they halted for two hours. But the fear of what could happen if they did not soon find water spurred them on, and they set off again, to march without another break until sundown. They made camp, slept fitfully, and rose yet again at first light, to march once more for seven hours without a break. And they came at length, not to the Khaba well, in the Dhafara, but to the one which al Auf had spoken of, the one at which his camel had refused to drink.

Such was their thirst, however, that the camels did not hesitate—at first. But after a few sips from the scummy liquid in the waterhole they withdrew, their hairy lips seeming to curl in monstrous disdain. Musallim had a little milk left in one of the goatskins. He mixed this with some water and, pinching the beast's nostrils in time-honored fashion, forced it to imbibe some of the liquid. The camel protested wildly, and the others did the same. But each at least wet its lips. The stench was awful. It even helped them to move swiftly on their next stage!

Twenty-four hours later the party reached the Khaba well, on the fringe of the Dhafara. It was December 12th. The worst of this terrible journey now lay behind them. Al Auf, that loyal Rashid Bedouin, could now assure Wilfred Thesiger that for the remainder of their journey to Liwa, though the going would continue to be hard and exacting, they need have no further fear of perishing from thirst in the lonely wastes of the Empty Quarter. And indeed, eventually this great crossing at what the Bedouin called, quite simply, the Sands, was achieved.

By the time he had completed his desert journey Thesiger had established the fact that locusts cannot breed in completely arid country. There must be some sort of vegetation, however sparse, if they are to lay their eggs and breed—and this, of course, is possible only when there has been at least some measure of rainfall. There was none in the Empty Quarter.

He therefore set out again, two years later, to survey another part of Arabia, actually the interior of Oman, on the east side that had been reported to have been the recipient of that rare gift: rain. He was not surprised to come across a number of isolated concentrations of locusts by the time he arrived there. Not only were there adult locusts, but there were a considerable number of what are known as "hoppers"—young locusts that had only recently been hatched from the eggs laid immediately after the rains.

His findings in 1948 and early 1949 sparked off researches on a very wide scale indeed, for locust swarms are a plague whose ravages have been suffered by man from Biblical times right up to the present day, and especially on the North African coast of the Mediterranean. A close watch is now maintained, internationally, on the breeding and migration of locusts and information collated on behalf of the Food and Agriculture Organization of the United Nations.

Peter Fleming in the Brazilian Jungle

Peter Fleming, traveler, former *London Times* Special Correspondent, military historian and brother of the late Ian (James Bond) Fleming, has performed some remarkable treks in the Far East and elsewhere, including Chinese Turkestan. One of the most remarkable of these journeys took place when he was a young man of twenty-five, in the year 1932.

He responded to an advertisement in *The Times* appealing for volunteers to join an expedition whose main objective was to search for one Colonel Fawcett who, seven years earlier, had mysteriously vanished—probably in the Mato Grosso region of Central Brazil—and of whom no trace had been found. But it was stated that this was to be a combined exploring and sporting expedition. As such, it had an immediate appeal, not only to Peter Fleming but to two former school and university friends who are named as Roger and Neville.

The expedition, organized on an elaborate scale for what was likely to prove a long and arduous journey through little-known and dangerous territory, sailed for Rio de Janeiro and then traveled by road to São Paulo and some eight hundred miles farther on into the interior until it came to the road's end at Leopoldina, on the River Araguaya. From there the party traveled by powered craft and subsequently by canoe for some four hundred miles northward through jungle territory to a point at which the major tributary, the Tapirape, joined the Araguaya. It was a strenuous

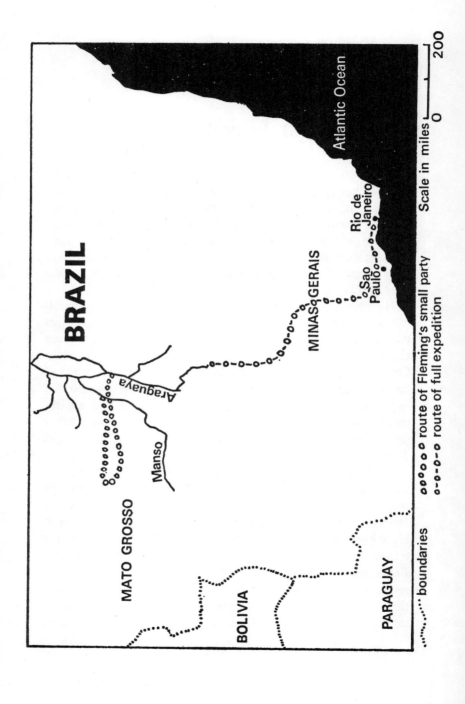

journey, not without hazards and problems, that occupied a full three weeks.

At the confluence of the two rivers the party branched off northwestward, up the smaller river. From its headwaters, some two hundred miles upstream, the intention was to do a cross-country trek southwestward in the direction of the River Kuluene, beyond the notorious Serra do Roncador, the area in which, it was believed, there would be the best chance of locating traces of the vanished colonel. But the party had not gone many miles up the Tapirape when the leader unexpectedly refused to go any farther, preferring to continue down the Araguaya to the Amazon Delta. Peter Fleming and his two friends, therefore, decided to continue on their own. They enlisted the services of a youthful one-eyed Brazilian named Queiroz, bade farewell to the rest of the party, and set off cheerfully enough on a journey that, they estimated, would be of at least a hundred and fifty miles out and the same distance back to base where, if they were lucky, the rest of the party would be waiting for them.

From the outset, Peter Fleming, who automatically assumed leadership of the breakaway expedition, recognized that without a native guide such an overland trek as they now contemplated would be impossible. Fortunately for them, two local tribesmen, who bore the same name as the river, Tapirapes, and whom they had encountered soon after leaving the Araguaya, seemed well disposed toward them. Bribed by presents of small mirrors, pocketknives, tobacco, and oddments such as used cartridge cases and by the promise of more substantial gifts to follow when their services were completed, they agreed to accompany the three Englishmen and Queiroz, the Brazilian. Their names were Camaira and Camarião, two brothers. The three Englishmen doubted from the start that they were reliable, but they had no option since none of the other Tapirape Indians appeared to be willing to leave the territory they knew for remote and probably hostile regions completely unknown to them.

Peter Fleming and his two companions weighed their chances without a great deal of optimism. The proposed trek would entail some three hundred miles, mainly through jungle territory; the notorious and little-known Mato Grosso began not many miles west of their starting point; the unexplored range of mountains named Serra do Roncador might well have to be negotiated. Also, the Chavante Indian tribe to the southwest—the general direction in which they were to be traveling—was well known to be traditionally hostile to the white man. It was unlikely in the extreme that the two Tapirapes would venture beyond the fringe of the Chavante territory. So, food and guides would have to be obtained from the Chavantes—a most unlikely prospect. The alternative was to live off the land, eating what they could shoot down. But the sound of their guns would most certainly alert, far in advance, Indian tribesmen occupying territory through which they would have to pass.

It was with this knowledge that toward the end of August the small party set out. The three white men were buoyed by enthusiasm rather than by optimism. Their Brazilian companion registered nothing. The two Tapirape Indians were silent from the outset. For the first few hours the going was unexpectedly easy. They marched over what was locally known as "campo," fairly level ground denuded of grass and other growth by systematic burning by the natives of the district, fellow-tribesmen of Camaira and Camarião. Fleming and his companions were a little disconcerted to note that these two men persisted in walking at their heels instead of ahead of them, as guides might be expected to do. But the party as a whole walked, on a compass-bearing, roughly south westward from the riverbank, the two Indians following them conscientiously whichever way their leader turned.

They came to a small river, their first true obstacle.

Camaira assured them that he knew of a good ford. This was the first, and almost the last time that he was to justify his presence as a so-called guide. He did in fact bring them to a point at which it was possible to cross the river. This was encouraging, but somehow Fleming and his two companions felt there was still little reason for optimism. They walked on, still over campo, but by now the jungle was beginning to close in on either side of them, and they knew that before long the two great masses of close-set trees would join, and they would then have no option but to plunge into it. In the meanwhile the only landmarks along the track they were following were the ant-hills, cones rising from the burnt ground to a yard or more. They were deserted, probably because of the systematic burning that had taken place in recent months. The party made a practice of lopping off their tops, rather in the way pioneers "blaze" a sequence of trees in order to mark the route taken so that they can follow it on their return.

Experience during the past weeks had shown that darkness fell in this area by about six o'clock in the evening. Shortly before nightfall they reached the outlyings of the true jungle. The trees and undergrowth were lush and green and implied that there was water nearby. Encouraged by the thought of water, they plunged into the trees. Soon the party was faced not only by close-set tree trunks, but by growths at their foot that were increasingly hard to penetrate. The shrubs that filled the space between each tree and its neighbor bore long, vicious thorns, their points sharp enough to pierce even the white men's clothing. They pierced even more deeply the bare legs and arms of the Indian guides. The two brothers now lagged farther and farther behind, complaining bitterly of the injuries they were receiving. Even though their language was unintelligible, it was quite evident that they were bitterly resentful of the ordeal they were being forced to undergo. It was a safe bet that at the first possible moment they would desert.

True, they had proved almost completely useless as guides, but the fact remained that they were carrying on their shoulders the entire stock of food supplies and much of the party's vital equipment. As carriers, if as nothing else, they had their uses!

They came at length to a patch of open ground that, surprisingly, evoked from Camarião the glad cry, *"Agua!"* There was no water in evidence, but now the Indian took charge. He took his machetelike knife, which the Brazilian Queiroz called a "facão," hacked a branch from a shrub, sharpened one end of it and drove it hard into the dried bed of what resembled a shallow pool. But even though each time he withdrew the stake and plunged it in again there was an encouraging sucking noise, there was no sign of moisture on the point, let alone of water. After a few minutes of half-hearted work Camarião threw away the stake, shrugged his shoulders and rejoined his brother who, from the first, had obviously not shared his belief that water might be found there. Its hopes shattered, the little party moved on in silence.

A little farther on they came to a second patch of dried-up mud among the trees. This time there was a layer of greenish slime in the center of it. The two Indians darted across to it, threw themselves down and plunged their mouths beneath the surface. As they broke through it, an obnoxious smell arose, compared with which the smell of bad eggs would be as fragrant as the scent of a flower. Queiroz followed suit, and the three white men watched to see what he would do. He dipped a mug into another part of the slime and extracted a small quantity. He tasted it, made a wry grimace, had a second taste, and then passed it over to Fleming.

The three men sampled it with extreme caution. Their joint verdict was that it resembled some rather farfetched kind of thin soup, but they realized at the same time that they were unquestionably swallowing a host of bacilli. What the result might be they hardly liked to contemplate. It seems rather strange that considering they were embarking on a long and strenuous overland trek, they did not take the elementary precaution of first boiling the stagnant water. Instead, they contented themselves with swallowing a tablet or two which, they had been assured before leaving England, would safeguard them against water poisoning. In fact, they do not seem to have suffered from this risky, even foolhardy, experiment in assuaging their thirst.

By now the trees were so thick overhead that they could not tell whether night had fallen or not. Their watches, however, told them that the hour of darkness was almost upon them. So they pressed on, believing that they must sooner or later break out of the trees and even find water. And their faith was rewarded. Marching in single file, the two Tapirape Indians steadfastly bringing up the rear, with Roger in the lead, they heard his excited cry, the blessed word "*Agua!*" Disregarding the thorns, they pressed on with increasing speed. Soon, to their enormous relief, their track dipped to the bank of a stream whose waters glistened beneath the now failing light of day. For the time being their anxieties were at an end.

They drank their fill. They cooked an evening meal. Then they turned in. But they did not sleep well. They had brought with them the minimum of blankets, not having expected to find that the nights in the jungle could be so cold. They had no mosquito nets, and the three white men suffered badly in consequence. This was one disadvantage in setting up camp on the bank of a river. The smoke from their campfire was of some use in checking the activities of these pests, but there was a fitful breeze and the smoke was wafted about so that they had continually to move around the fire if they were to get the benefit of it. They were very tired. Roger, who was handiest with compass and navigating generally, calculated that they had covered some fifteen miles in all. That might be called reasonably good going, in view of the conditions they had encountered, but this was only one tenth, at best, of the total outward trek that they believed awaited them.

As they cooked a simple breakfast the next morning they realized, from the behavior of the two Tapirape Indians, that something was afoot. Very soon they were to know what it was. Camarião was their spokesman. They had come, he announced, as far as they were prepared to come. They were now on the fringe of territory unknown to them. Beyond this point they would be approaching that of the Chavantes. They had suffered grievously from the poisonous jungle thorns. In brief—and all this was made clear in a gabble of unintelligible words illuminated by unmistakable gestures, such as pointing to the scars on their legs and registering fear of the territory and its dreaded inhabitants —they had decided to turn back here and now. They had placed the packs they had been carrying on the ground at their feet. That at any rate was something—they might, after all, have absconded with them during the night!

On the whole, Fleming and his companions were relieved to learn that their so-called guides were going to defect. From the start they had not felt much confidence in them. They had really been useful only as carriers of loads. In the circumstances, they were very well treated. Fleming took his .22 repeating rifle and went off and shot five large birds, of a species known as "jacu." These he presented to the two Indians to sustain them on their return journey to their homes on the banks of the Tapirape. The two men received the unexpected gift with grunts of satisfaction, but were less pleased when they found that they were to be their sole reward. Fleming contrived to make it clear that they had been paid handsomely in advance. The balance was to have been paid to them when the trek was successfully accomplished.

Neville took another gun and went off in search of food

for their own larder. He took a potshot at a large fish that surfaced near at hand, a barbado of fierce expression made all the stranger by the set of side-whiskers with which it is equipped and from which, presumably, it derives its name "the bearded one." Rather to his surprise, he shot it dead in such a way that its spasmodic leap-in-death took it right onto the riverbank. They cut four steaks from it and roasted these over the fire. To wash it down, they drank cocoa, brewed from two bars of chocolate that had melted in one of the packs during the heat of the previous day's march and was in consequence fit for nothing else. Then, their odd meal finished, they dowsed their campfire and made ready to start sorting the loads they would now have to carry on their own shoulders.

It was while they were doing this that Fleming became conscious that all was not well with Neville. He was struggling, with a look of anguish on his face, to pull on his boots. Suddenly, with a gesture of mingled fury and despair, he blurted out in one bleak phrase, "Sorry. No can do." Several weeks before, at the beginning of their canoe trip down the Araguaya, he had blistered his feet in a pair of new boots. The blisters had turned septic, and poison had entered his bloodstream. He had been anxious about the state of his feet even before this small party had severed connection with the others, but had manfully said nothing about his trouble, hoping that with steady use, and the application of medicaments at the end of each day, the sores would improve and the poison pass from his system. Probably in his heart of hearts he had known all along that this was a forlorn hope. His feet had become increasingly painful with every furlong covered.

A quick decision was called for. As leader of the party, Fleming made it. Clearly, there was no question as to Neville's accompanying them any farther. He must return to base at once. If he left now, without a moment's delay, he could overtake the two Tapirapes and travel back with them to the river. There one or more of the expedition's boats would still be tied up, for the original leader had said that he proposed to linger there for some time before proceeding back down the Araguaya to Para, near the mouth of the Amazon.

Neville of course was bitterly disappointed. But he knew perfectly well that it would be folly to try to continue. Not only would it be an exhausting and possibly fatal journey for himself, but he would almost certainly become a liability and a drag on his companions. Into his mind there flashed the memory of Captain Oates, a member of Scott's Polar Expedition who, rather than allow his own weakness to make him a drag on the rest of the party, had deliberately gone out into the blizzard to die there alone.

Camaira and his brother Camarião had not long been gone. Neville made a supreme effort to force his feet into his boots, bade an almost silent goodbye to his two friends, and set off in pursuit of them. His bottle had been filled with fresh water and he had his quota of food necessary for one day's journey back to the river. When he had vanished into the trees, Fleming, Roger Pettiward and the one-eyed Brazilian Queiroz began once more, and in silence, to make preparations to continue their trek southwestward.

The first thing to do was to make careful appraisal of what they now had to divide among the three of them. To begin with, they were quite well armed. They had the .22 repeating rifle, a .44 rifle with a small amount of ammunition, a .45 service revolver with some thirty rounds of ammunition, and two facões. They could not make out why they had only two, not three, of these indispensable knives, a combined weapon and tool without which no man in his senses would ever confront jungle conditions. Possibly one or other of the Tapirape Indians had secretly appropriated the third one. This was unlikely, for the Tapirapes have an

IN THE BRAZILIAN JUNGLE

unusual reputation for honesty. However, the fact remained that the three men had among them only two of these knives with which to face the many miles of jungle that undoubtedly lay ahead of them.

Their food supply was meager, for they had set out resolved to live off the land, knowing that they could not carry a great deal with them. They had a few pounds of porridge oats, less than a pound in all of malted milk powder, a couple of tins of biscuits, a few bars of chocolate that, as they had already found to their cost, had stood up badly to the heat and humidity and was really fit for nothing except boiling into a few drinks of cocoa.

In addition, however, they had a reasonable supply of a commodity known as "farinha." This was a coarse type of flour made from grinding up a mandioca root after the poisonous fluid in it had been carefully extracted. It could be mixed with almost anything, but added bulk rather than palatability to what it was mixed with. But with supplies as scarce as they were, even though it added to the overall weight that now had to be distributed among the three of them, they could not afford to throw this farinha away. One other food item appeared in this scanty larder. It was a substance somewhat resembling toffee that went by the name of "rapadura." A little of this—provided your teeth were your own, and were in good condition—went a very long way indeed! The heaviest individual package they had with them was a large bag of salt. They had been told before the expedition set out that this was much prized by Brazilian Indian tribes and was well worth carrying for use as payment for services rendered.

So the three men divided their supplies into three loads, as equal as possible. Packed into one rucksack, one ex-army haversack, and one nondescript canvas bag, most of what they had to carry could be accommodated. What was left over had to be crammed into pockets or slung about them with lengths of twine. They jettisoned anything they felt they could spare, with the vague notion that perhaps on their return journey, if they came this way, they could pick it up again.

Rather than turn back into the jungle again, they decided to follow the river upstream for a while, since its direction was near to that which they had laid down for their route towards the Kuluene. With luck, they told themselves, the going should be easier along a riverbank than among the trees and treacherous undergrowth with which they had had to contend during the previous afternoon and evening. Certainly at times it did prove to be easier. Often they covered several hundred yards close alongside the water's edge with very little difficulty. But every now and then they would come to a stretch of riverbank that was made indescribably treacherous by the intertwining roots of trees and shrubs twisting this way and that through the earth and threatening to trip them so that they fell headlong into the fast-running water. And for all they knew there were jacares, Brazilian alligators, in that water, and arrayas, sinister fresh-water stingrays with barbed tails so deadly that some Indian tribes use them for tipping their arrows. They had seen enough of what poison could do, in their friend's bloodstream, to be unwilling to take that sort of risk themselves, unless there was absolutely no alternative.

The river was shallow. From time to time they waded across it from one bank to the other, partly because the going always seemed more promising on the far side, though it did not always prove to be so. Partly, also, because they hoped in that way to be able to cut off some of the more extravagant winds of the river course. They well knew that to follow a river instead of steering a direct compass-course was to multiply their actual mileage by two or three or even more. On the other hand, when close alongside the river they could at least see roughly where they were heading, whereas in the heart of the jungle, even at high noon, they often had to rely on a mixture of compass and pure guesswork.

The second day out alternated between slogging through stretches of near-impenetrable jungle, swinging their facões left and right until their arms ached and blisters rose on the palms of their hands, and tramping alongside the serpentining river. In the open, and as the hour advanced to midday, the heat became increasingly hard to bear. When they turned, for a change, into the jungle itself, there was no longer the direct heat of the sun on their heads and shoulders, but the hot and sticky humidity of an enclosed space that had never known sunshine or breeze and soon became as unbearable as the direct beams of the sun. There was no breeze whatsoever to fan their perspiring foreheads; it was like walking continuously alongside a row of furnaces.

Peter Fleming was a crack shot, and soon he had brought down a small deer known as a "veado." This was, of course, a wasteful mode of catering, for they could not possibly carry more than a small part of the beast since they were already more than heavily loaded. In any case, in this humid heat flesh soon became uneatable. So they contented themselves with removing the veado's liver, as a delicacy, and a good chunk of solid meat from one haunch.

The three men slept, that second night, by their campfire on the riverbank, with the edge of the jungle immediately behind them. They speculated as to whether by night there might be jungle animals on the prowl—jaguars, for instance. They therefore drew up a system of watch-keeping. Reckoning that there would be about ten hours of darkness, they agreed that each should stay awake and on the alert for a three-hour spell while the two others slept. He would also maintain the campfire, for wild animals were known to fear flames. On the other hand, as Fleming remarked, the light of the fire would almost certainly attract any wandering tribesmen, and these would now be Chavantes, for they had reached their territory. They slept ill, that second night.

There were the unceasing attacks of the mosquitoes, the incessant metallic racket of the armies of cicadas, and innumerable unidentifiable noises.

Before setting out the next day they debated seriously the alternatives that were open to them if they were to cover the great stretch of difficult terrain that lay ahead of them. It was Fleming who came up with a third alternative to the two methods they had tried so far. He found the water was very much shallower near the camp than it had been, for the river had widened considerably. What, he asked the others, was to prevent them from using the actual river as their route, wading through water instead of forcing their way through jungle or undergrowth?

They struck camp, loaded their gear as high as possible on their shoulders, and set off in single file upstream. It proved to be a strange experience. For perhaps twenty yards they would be walking on a gritty, sandy riverbed. They had to lean forward all the time in order to breast the slow-flowing water. Then, suddenly, the riverbed would seem to drop away. Instead of walking waist deep, they would find the water up to their armpits, even up to their necks. Whoever was in the lead would cast about him for a part of the river that was less deep, making his way toward the bank that was the nearer at the time.

At least, though, in the river they were clear of the tangled undergrowth of the jungle, with its vicious and inescapable thorns. Forward movement, against the stream, involved steady muscular effort, but at least they could always see what sort of progress they were making. In the jungle, on the other hand, however great their efforts, it often seemed to them that they were making no real progress at all. True, in midstream as the sun rose to its zenith it beat down on them pitilessly, but at least they had relatively cool water flowing past them, and they could wash their foreheads from time to time and take a welcome drink of water very much cooler than that contained in their flasks.

They did not need to remind each other that by following the river all the time they were probably multiplying their mileage by three times or more. But on the whole the advantages outweighed the disadvantages and they were making slow, if tortuous, progress. But there was one ever-present problem—they simply had to know the general direction in which they were traveling. An occasional glance at the sun was not sufficient to establish their line of march; the compass must be continuously observed, a note made of every change of direction and a note, too, of the approximate distance traveled between each turn and the last. Only by doing this consistently could they hope to maintain progress generally in the right direction and to fill in a chart, however rough, of the route they were taking. They had to bear in mind all the time the fact that they must find their way back to base again when their outward trek was completed.

Of the three men, Queiroz was easily the smallest, though he made up for this by being both muscular and wiry. It was height, or the lack of it, that mattered when a sudden increase in the depth of water, due to a hollow in the riverbed, was encountered. The first accident of the day occurred when the Brazilian dropped suddenly into what must have been a riverbed pot-hole and momentarily vanished from sight. He was never allowed to take the lead, for obvious reasons, and for most of the time it was Roger Pettiward, the tallest of the three, who led the way upstream. Perhaps due allowance had not been made for the little Brazilian. In any case, he vanished suddenly, though he bobbed up fairly quickly by stepping backward with the flow of water to assist him. But the damage had been done. It happened that he was carrying the main load of the essential farinha. That brief ducking ruined it completely. At one blow, this basic element in their poverty-stricken larder ceased to exist.

It was just after midday. They had been breasting the waters of this small river ever since striking camp some five hours before, and this seemed as good a moment as any to scramble ashore and prepare some sort of a meal. The sun was blazing down, so this would give them the chance to dry out their sodden clothes. They stripped and spread their garments on the bushes to dry. Roger, who had suffered more than his companions from the attacks of the mosquitoes during the night, owing to having torn his bush-shirt and jacket, lay down and was instantly asleep. Queiroz lit a cigar which he had kept dry in a wrapper of oiled silk, shut his eyes and appeared to go into some kind of a trance. Fleming speculated as to whether it was pure tobacco that he was smoking, or some stronger form of narcotic.

As for himself, he placed on record that for him this day was the high spot, so far, of their trek. He watched a kingfisher, a species very much smaller than those he had been used to seeing on rivers at home, and differently colored. It had an orange breast, dark-green back and wings, a black head and a strikingly white ruff—like, he remarked, a medieval page boy in a brand-new livery. Roger and Queiroz were fast asleep still, but he felt restless. He picked up his gun and wandered along the riverbank and then actually a little way into the jungle, though wisely he did not penetrate for more than a few yards. He was wearing boots, but nothing else. The thorny scrub soon brought him to a halt. He looked about him. It was as he did so that he heard the unmistakable sound of a snapping twig. His mind turned instantly to the thought of a roving Indian. Then, with boyhood memories flooding in of the genius that Indians have for traveling without making a sound, he dismissed the momentary thought of a lone encounter with a roving Chavante tribesman, and speculated as to what was on the move, unseen yet so close to him. It proved to be a small veado. This reminded him that his party required something for lunch. He put his rifle to his shoulder, shot the creature accurately through the neck, snapping its spinal column so that it fell dead instantly. Back at the riverbank, he woke

Queiroz, and between them they carved off sufficient meat for a meal right away and another when they pitched camp later on at the end of the day.

Their strength restored by the succulent veado steaks, they set off again, plunging upstream through the gently flowing water. The sun was almost full in their eyes, so they knew they were still traveling generally in the right direction. But it was as well that they had recouped some of their strength, for they came soon to a stretch of water where Fate seemed to have turned against them. The trees and undergrowth now spread right down to the water's edge on both banks. Their roots, and the lianas and straggling, thorn-equipped branches of some of the riotous shrubs, reached out from either side and practically linked twigs in midstream. So, they now had the worst of both worlds. They might as well have remained in the jungle, or on the riverbank, where at least they would not have had to compete against the pressure of the flowing stream and the uncertainty of the riverbed.

It was the most exhausting two hours' traveling they had had to accomplish to date. Moreover, the interlacing roots beneath the surface, often reaching right down to the riverbed itself, housed infinite numbers of small fish. Some of these, Queiroz reminded them, could be the deadly black piranha. This is a notorious Brazilian fish capable, so it is said, of attacking in shoals and stripping a victim to bare bone in a matter of minutes. But by then the three men were too weary to think seriously of what a shoal of piranhas could do. They simply struggled on in silence, their one aim being to make what progress they could and find a suitable campsite in which to rest when darkness fell.

They at length found a site, and thankfully gave up traveling for that day. The first thing they did was to collect brushwood and light a fire, for this was the only way of warding off the incessant waves of ferocious mosquitoes that haunted the riverbanks and undergrowth and swarmed out in their millions as soon as darkness fell. Roger, with his badly torn clothing, had been kept awake most of the previous night by their attacks and did not fancy a second night as bad as the last one. They cooked a meal of fish, including a huge, bewhiskered barbado that they had caught by the primitive method of spearing it with a sharpened stake. One vital accessory they had not had the forethought to bring with them was a fishing-line and hooks.

It was during the late evening that they became aware of a fire burning at some distance from them. It was obviously not just a campfire, but one on a huge scale. They supposed it must be another stretch of campo being burned by the Indians. Queiroz said he was pretty sure they were now on the edge of Chavante territory, and his statement did not add to their sense of security. Nor were they happy at the realization that the fire seemed to be sweeping rapidly in their direction. They tried to work out whether their camp lay actually in its path, but even the compass did not help them here. In the end they came to the conclusion that though it was obviously coming in their direction, it was probably on the other side of the river. The river, small as it was, should serve as a useful firebreak. But there was still the worry that the Indians responsible for the fire, and jealous, as ever, of their territorial rights, were probably Chavantes.

Not surprisingly, the three men slept fitfully that night, their problems racing around in their minds and no satisfactory answer to them emerging. But over a light breakfast the next morning the leader of the expedition decided what they must now do. The rate of their progress was to some extent handicapped by the small stature of the Brazilian. In any case, they possessed only two facões among the three of them, and the previous day's traveling had shown how utterly essential it was for each member of the party to be individually equipped.

So, Fleming now suggested that Queiroz should be left at

this campsite, with the whole of the food supply and all the rest of the gear, save for a few "iron ration," the two facões and one gun. He and Roger Pettiward would set out on a brisk foray to ascertain the lay of the land in the area immediately ahead of them. They would return by nightfall to rejoin Queiroz, and in the light of what they had discovered, would then decide on their next step as a party. The Brazilian lit another cigar, grinned his friendly grin and, quite unperturbed, watched their departure with his one good eye.

The day was to have a surprising end, folowing a succession of surprises. The two men had not progressed very far when, to their relief, the jungle began to thin out. They came to a stretch of campo, and wondered whether perhaps they had done the right thing in leaving Queiroz behind them, for he would make as good progress here as they themselves could. Had they better turn about and collect him, they asked each other. But something prompted them to continue on their way, following their first instinct.

They marched southwestward for a while over this easier terrain. They found it difficult to judge distances, however. This was partly because of the heat haze and partly because of the smoke from the burning campo far ahead of them that lay almost motionless a little above treetop height. Theoretically, the range of mountains known as the Serra do Roncador should by now have come within view. Strangely, though, there was no sign of the mountains. So far as they could judge in the haze, the terrain was flat right to the horizon. But the question that puzzled them was, how far distant was that horizon? They found it quite impossible to judge.

After a while they came to an isolated clump of trees, outliers, at a guess, of an area of jungle that had been destroyed by a more than ordinarily devastating man-made fire. The trees looked to be about sixty feet tall. So they laid down their gear and began, painfully and laboriously, to climb as high as possible the tallest of the trees. The idea was, that having reached a height of sixty feet or so, they would be able to see very much farther along their route than they could from ground level. But the effort proved to be more trouble than it was worth. They could certainly see much farther than they had been able to, but the looked-for mountain range that was to have given them their bearings was still, mysteriously, non-existent.

As they climbed down again, disappointed, they speculated about this. They had not been able to obtain any really accurate-looking maps before their departure from São Paulo. In fact, inquiry had revealed that the area they were proposing to explore had never been accurately charted. So perhaps the Serra do Roncador was nothing more than a figment of some cartographer's imagination, a feature that he inserted in the map because he felt there just *ought* to be a mountain range somewhere there? As they stepped back from the foot of the tree they had just climbed, they felt that they had expended a great deal of valuable energy to no purpose whatsoever.

They stood there awhile, pondering their next move, looking first in the direction they had been intending to take and then back over the route they had followed since leaving Queiroz. He had undertaken to keep the campfire going and to feed it with wet branches so that it would send up an unmistakable pillar of smoke into the still air. This would enable them to keep their bearings and would be of assistance when the time came to turn back and rejoin him. He was, they noted with relief, doing his job conscientiously. The pillar of smoke was rising straight into the sky, like a giant exclamation mark hanging in space.

But they had hardly resumed their march before they realized that apart from the major fire on the distant campo, there was now another fire, more of the type that the Brazilian was keeping alight. Less than a mile ahead of them, another great column of smoke had suddenly shot into the sky, lit on its underside by the lurid light of what must be a huge fire. It was, obviously, no chance-lit forest fire. It was without question an Indians' answer to Queiroz's camp-signal fire, an unmistakable challenge. The Chavantes, it was now obvious to the two men, knew of their presence—and were letting them know that they knew. It seemed to be the right moment to turn around and rejoin Queiroz, and think again.

It was nearly dark by the time they reached camp. Queiroz had speared two fish, and they ate hungrily. But it was an uneasy group that sat around the fire that evening, and for a very good reason. Fires seemed to have started up all about them. The wind had risen, as it tended to do around nightfall, and some of the fires seemed to be closing in on them dangerously fast. There was always the river, of course, as a refuge, but here it was no longer wide and shallow but was running close-confined and narrow between unusually steep banks. It was certainly too deep to wade through, so that if they had to make use of it as an escape route they would have to swim, somehow keeping their sadly diminished stock of food clear of the water. Even more important, they must preserve their rifles intact, and their ammunition.

They were still debating their chances and prospects, which had now so evidently taken a turn for the worse, when the wholly unexpected happened. With the suddenness that is characteristic of tropical rainstorms in many parts of the world, the heavens opened and rain fell.

But this was no ordinary rain. Queiroz might well have experienced it before, but it was unlike any rain that Fleming and his companion had ever known. It was tropical rain. It did not so much pour down in vertical lines, or sheets, as flood down. It had the weight of the water which they had been breasting for days on end as they forced their way upstream. It was a river flowing against them, not horizontally but vertically, with crushing weight.

Within the first minute they were all three soaked to the

skin and shivering, for this rain was, unexpectedly, icy cold. Its impact was made more unbearable by the fury of the wind, that increased with every passing minute. There was something diabolical in its power. It gave the impression of being impelled by human volition, of being determined to destroy everything that stood in its path. The noise it made was deafening. It struck the surface of the river with the force of grape-shot. The air was filled with sound so intense that the men thought their eardrums would burst. The earth beneath their feet seemed to be screaming in some sort of agony. The three men, cowering beside their now extinguished campfire, felt themselves to be a part of that universal agony.

Queiroz jerked them by the elbows and made a dive for a hollow beneath the roots of a tree close by. The cavity was hardly large enough to contain more than one of them, but somehow all three of them managed to crowd into it, at least their bodies, though their legs remained outside, savagely attacked by the mass of falling water.

How long the storm lasted they did not know. One hour? Two hours? Three? In the darkness, and in that hurly-burly of furious sound they had lost all count of time. Then, as suddenly as it had started, it ceased. It was as though a gigantic tap in the heavens above had been decisively turned off. The wind, too, had ceased. There was an eerie silence all about them. Emerging from their makeshift shelter, they looked about them, staring into the darkness. Where there had been light from the great jungle fires that had been burning when they returned to camp, now there was only thick, impenetrable darkness. That tropical rainstorm had effectively extinguished the flames that only a few hours earlier had threatened to engulf them.

Their ears were still singing from the tumult they had had to endure. Fleming and his companion looked at one another with raised eyebrows. This, they realized, was the moment of truth. All now became crystal clear to them. It was the end of August. Ordinarily, in that part of South America, the major rains did not commence until October. But the consensus of opinion in São Paulo before they left for the Araguaya and the Tapirape, with the Kuluene as their objective, was that this year the rains were almost certain to commence sometime in September. During the rainy season no one, save the true jungle dwellers, could survive in the jungle. Certainly no white man could. Quite apart from their ferocity, and the consequent problems of swollen rivers and flooded low-lying campo, these rains invariably brought disease in their wake.

These were hard, inescapable facts. That storm, Peter Fleming and Roger Pettiward strongly suspected, was but the forerunner of other deluges to come, of those everlengthening periods of storm that constitute the annual rainy season. And there were other inescapable facts. Even if the Chavantes could be bribed with gifts to abandon their traditional hostility and offer them food and their services as guides, in circumstances like these it would be suicide to rely on them. After all, Camaira and his brother, both members of a so-called friendly tribe, had proved a dead loss.

Then there was the question of their own food stocks. They had left to them one tin of oatmeal, a few ounces of malted milk powder, an ounce or two of tea, a lump or two of rapadura, and a hideous residue at the bottom of one pack, consisting of mixed farinha, some chocolate, some biscuit fragments and grains of salt. Their supply of ammunition, too, was running low. If their rifles had been badly affected by the torrential rain they might no longer be reliable. All in all, the prospect was bleak.

It is not necessarily cowardice that makes a man turn back, his objective unachieved; it can even be a certain type of courage. It was courage that prompted the decision that Peter Fleming, as leader of this three-man expedition in search of the vanished Colonel Fawcett, was now obliged to make. Had he been on his own, he might have come to a different decision, but the fact remained that he was responsible for the safety of the Brazilian Queiroz, who was in his employ. And whereas he himself had volunteered for this expedition, he had brought gentle pressure on his friend Roger to throw in his lot with them.

Roger Pettiward was not surprised at the decision made, for he knew the integrity of his old school friend. He knew at heart that the decision to turn back was the right one. Had he himself been leader he would have made it. As for Queiroz, he was always a man of very few words. Certainly he was not sorry. Better than either of the others he knew what the rainy season could mean in the dark heart of his own country.

They gathered up their sodden packs and turned about. As they did so, the largest jacare they had seen during the whole of their wanderings nosed its way toward the bank on which they had pitched camp and lit the fire that was now just a blackened mass of waterlogged embers. The jacare was swimming in the very water through which the three men had been struggling upstream only the previous day. Fleming picked up his trusty .22 rifle, loaded it, took aim, and shot the loathsome-looking creature through its one truly vulnerable spot, its eye. It gave a convulsive heave halfway out of the water, seeming almost to stand for a dramatic moment on its armor-plated tail. Then, slowly, it slid backward beneath the surface. Perhaps the shooting of the jacare was a gesture of defiance against Fate, which had decided against their continuing this trek into the Mato Grosso. The waters closed over the corpse, and at the same time the three men entered the jungle, and the trees and undergrowth closed in about them as they began their long, laborious journey back to their starting point.

The expedition which Peter Fleming joined was by no means the only one that searched for traces of Colonel Fawcett, but all of them failed. This is not surprising, for the territory into which he disappeared in 1925 was, and remains, among the most impenetrable and dangerous on the whole surface of the globe.

So—the truth as to his vanishing remains a mystery. Whole books have been written about him, but every one of them ends, inevitably, in mere speculation. That he is dead is of course now certain, for if he were to be alive today he would be well over a hundred years old—and no man lives to that sort of age, even in the easiest of circumstances, in the heart of the Mato Grosso.

Dervla Murphy
from Ireland to India

In January, 1963, a thirty-year-old Irishwoman set out to fulfil a girlhood dream—to bicycle from her home in County Waterford to Delhi, in India. She faced a journey of several thousand miles, but as she pointed out to friends who told her she was mad even to consider doing it, "the way to India offered fewer watery obstacles than any other destination at a similar distance."

The real start of her long journey awheel was of course in France, after she had crossed the Irish Sea and the English Channel by boat. From Dunkirk onward, she and her beloved and trusty bicycle, "Roz," were on their own. "Roz," perhaps, was an echo of the name "Rosinante" which Don Quixote gave to the horse that led him through so many strange adventures. Now, she and Roz had the whole of Europe to cross—then Turkey, then Persia, then Afghanistan, then West Pakistan. There would be desert country and there would be mountain roads and passes, many of them infested with bandits, where even experienced men traveled in convoy rather than on their own, for protection.

Dervla Murphy was of course well aware of all this. But she was a determined person, and as her great trek was to prove over the long months that followed, an indomitable one. She completed her marathon journey. Her diary shows that she averaged between seventy and eighty miles on every day that she was in the saddle. She never covered less than twenty miles, and frequently, even in what many cyclists would be tempted to call "impossible" country, she covered as much as a hundred miles and more—good going even on roads with good surfaces. The overall journey occupied almost exactly six eventful months. Perhaps the most consistently eventful stage was that of some six hundred miles between Tehran, in Persia (which we know today as Iran) and the Persian-Afghan frontier at Ghurion, which she reached just nine days later.

It was six-thirty on the morning of March 31st when she swung into the saddle. She had been told by the authorities in Tehran that it was entirely out of the question for anyone—least of all a woman—to cycle across Persia and on into Afghanistan. Such a thing, they assured her, never had been done and never would be done. Rather than disappoint her, they would be happy to find her a place in some motorized convoy traveling eastward, and even to cover her expenses at least as far as Kabul, the capital of Afghanistan and springboard for the notorious Khyber Pass, which she would have later to climb.

This was a generous gesture on their part. But Dervla Murphy was a very resolute woman indeed. She firmly declined all their offers, with thanks. She had, she pointed out, come all that way on her bicycle, and was determined to complete the long journey by cycle which had been a dream ever since, at the age of ten, she had been given her first machine, and at the same time her first atlas. These gifts combined had inspired her to attempt this mammoth journey, and it was too late to stop her now. Somehow she wheedled her way around their objections, and as so often both before and afterwards, got her own way.

To begin with on this stage, luck was with her. As though anxious to demonstrate that she had been right to insist, the wind changed from east to west and now blew so strongly that on her first day out of Tehran she covered well over a hundred miles in less than twelve hours' pedaling. And she was not traveling light, either. In addition to the essen-

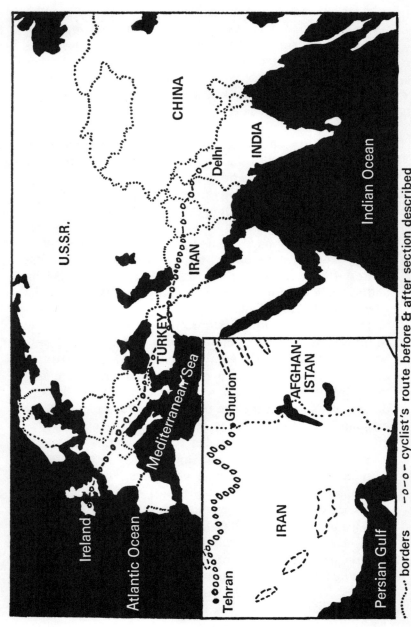

tial change of clothing she carried, she had a fairly comprehensive first-aid kit, a pistol and ammunition (which she hoped never to have to use), a number of route maps, notebooks and ballpoint pens, camping equipment, and a number of spare inner-tubes, brake-cables and lamp batteries. All this weighed something in excess of thirty-five pounds and was packed into two baskets and a saddlebag. She had sent on in advance to various British Consulates a supply of spare tires, for she had no illusions as to the conditions she she would have to encounter on the roads once she had reached Eastern Europe and countries beyond, like Turkey.

The early stages of her journey through Persia eastward from Tehran were relatively easy going. It was mostly agricultural land, well tended by peasants who lived in the mud-hut villages scattered along each side of the road. Whenever she stopped she was immediately surrounded by hordes of small children, and many grownups too, astonished at seeing a young woman alone on a bicycle on a road that carried only herds of cattle and convoys of trucks. Her regular practice, on arrival near nightfall at any village, was to make for the local police barracks. There she was almost invariably made welcome and offered a simple cell-like room and a shakedown for the night. Sometimes the room was larger, and she had to share it with others. More often than not her bed-fellows were fleas and other insects that permanently occupied the premises in vast numbers. In course of time she became as accustomed to these pests as the natives themselves, and almost ceased to notice their presence.

So strong was the sun that she had long developed the habit of rising at first light and setting off without delay to cover as much ground as possible before the heat became unbearable. On her second day out of Tehran she left the police barracks at half-past five in the morning, in the cool half-light of dawn. The road had deteriorated badly, and though she succeeded in covering some eighty miles, this took her thirteen grueling hours, allowing for an hour's halt at midday when cycling became impossible. Unfortunately there was no shade except a few thornbushes, and she became badly sunburned. This surprised her, because she had come to believe that by then she was sufficiently inured to both sun and wind. This sunburn was to prove a major problem for a long while to come.

After her midday break the road, though the police had described it as a main road, deteriorated so badly that she found she could progress more easily along the bed of a dried-up river which ran alongside. This offered her hard-baked mud and an occasional boulder to negotiate, but even this was likely to prove less damaging to her tires than the flinty gravel that formed the surface of the so-called road. So, she alternately cycled and pushed her faithful Roz for ten long miles on this riverbed before returning to the road. This became necessary when the riverbed slanted away from her true course so much that to keep to it could mean doubling the length of that stage of her journey.

The reason for this divergence of road and river soon became apparent. The road began to climb the western slopes of some high hills, and for the remaining thirty miles of that long day she was climbing on a gradient just too steep to ride without extreme effort but not always steep enough to warrant pushing her machine. It was, in fact, a notorious stretch of road. Only a few days before she had cycled and walked over it, a truck and a local bus crammed with passengers and their belongings had met head-on part way around a hairpin turn. The impact had hurled both vehicles off the road and headlong into a dry ravine a hundred feet below. All fifty passengers and both drivers had been killed.

Dervla Murphy did not actually witness this accident, but in the space of ten days she witnessed no fewer than seven road accidents, in which a number of people were killed, or hideously maimed, before her shocked eyes. It was an unnerving experience, and it says much for the courage and persistence of this young Irishwoman that it did not deter her from completing her long journey. And she knew, too, that the farther east she went the more hazardous the roads were certain to become.

The next day, the road degenerated into a mere track. It took her thirteen hours of hard slogging to cover a bare sixty miles. Of those sixty miles, she reckoned that she walked, pushing her heavily loaded bicycle, more than twenty. From time to time she was forced to leave the track and seek cover on one side or the other as trucks, overloaded with freight and passengers they were never intended to carry, complete with an unimaginable assortment of belongings, including crates of poultry, lambs, kids (four-legged as well as human), suitcases, rolled-up blankets and rugs, and broken-down bicycles and miscellaneous cooking utensils, rumbled and roared and lurched past her, threatening with every turn of their wheels to jettison their crazy cargoes. How they stayed on such a track was a miracle.

Toward the end of this grueling day she began to be seriously worried about her right arm. It was, of course, the one that was chiefly exposed to the sun in the south, as she was riding eastward. It had by now swollen badly, for she had rather foolishly omitted to smear it with the sunburn lotion she carried in her first-aid kit. The swollen arm was to cause her more and more pain for many days to come, and she was very conscious of the fact that cycling all day and sleeping rough by night presented a grave risk of blood-poisoning when the blisters broke and revealed the tender skin beneath. And this was bound to happen before long.

On the fourth day of this stage through Persia she had to break her strict rule not to ride after nightfall because of the risk of unseen dangers. The simple fact was that the road had become so bad that in order to cover the eighty-odd miles she had set herself to reach her chosen destination she had to keep pedaling away until half-past nine that night, well after sundown. And she was now riding in what was virtually desert country. There were sand dunes, like low hills, stretching to the horizon on either side of the road. Their shadows were strong, and beautifully shaped to the contours of their crests and folds, and the contrast between black and white became stronger as the full moon shone down upon them at an angle.

The road was completely deserted now that darkness had fallen. Now and then she thought she could make out a tiny pinpoint of light, perhaps from some isolated mud hut, but she could never be sure. You might think that she would have been feeling desperately lonely on this empty road, crossing a near-desert beneath a vast sky, but she was not. She wrote afterward of this stretch of cycling by moonlight as being among the most memorable of her experiences. Earlier on, she had been overtaken on the road by the driver of a jeep who first offered her a lift and then, because she turned down his offer, drove on angrily shouting back over his shoulder that she must be a "nut-case." Some other people, including the authorities at Tehran, may have been tempted to think that that is what she was, but to read her complete story is to realize that this is very far from being the truth.

Roz, however, was now showing signs of wear and tear. Both mudguards had gone, and the rear-lamp bracket had snapped off. The straps holding her saddlebag to the saddle had broken, and one of the baskets had come adrift from its mounting. Worse, there was clearly something amiss with the right pedal. It was hardly surprising, for every part of her machine, frame and fittings alike, had been subjected for the past three months to continuous vibration on roads that seemed to be deteriorating with every mile covered.

At the village she came to, after darkness had fallen and at the end of that long and hard day's pedaling, there was no police barracks. The village consisted of nothing more than a cluster of the usual mud huts, grouped about a central "tea-house" that had a counter of mud and a mud bench running around the inside of three walls. A ramshackle wooden stairway rose from the beaten-earth floor to an upper room. Here she hoped to find sleeping accommodation. Perhaps it was, but it seemed to be occupied entirely by a number of men smoking opium pipes and already so far under the influence of the drug that not one of them even noticed her entry.

Though her right arm was now so stiff and intensely painful that she could hardly use it, she managed to drag her bicycle up the steps. She made it fast to her wrist with a strap, then laid her head on the saddlebag as a pillow and passed out for the night, oblivious of everything that was going on all around her. Because of the acute pain in her swollen arm, which felt as if it was on fire, she slept only fitfully. Each time she woke, surrounded by the snores of unseen opium smokers, it was still pitch dark. At five o'clock she could rest no longer. She got up from her uncomfortable baked-mud mattress, stumbled awkwardly down the steps, dragging Roz with her, and emerged into the open, where at least the air was fit to breathe. There was no one else about. Stiffly, she swung her leg over the saddle and set off in the early morning light.

Her route for the whole of the day's ride lay through part of the so-called Great Salt Desert. Sand stretched in unbroken waves to the far horizon on both sides of the track she had to follow. The only township she passed through during the whole of that interminable day was a squalid place called Salzevar. She approached with some apprehension, for she had heard some days before that it was the scene of incessant strife between two religious sects, both of which were so hostile toward authority that the local police had given up all hope of controlling them, and simply moved out of the district.

Dervla Murphy felt the effects of the situation almost at once. She had hardly entered Salzevar before groups of loud-voiced youths wearing green turbans and shouting slogans attacked her with a hail of stones and other missiles. The road passed through the center of the place, and she had no alternative but to follow it. Some of the stones were sharp, and their impact burst several of the blisters on her burned right arm. This hurt so much that she had to grit her teeth even to maintain her hold on the handlebars. She made what speed she could, for no one came to her aid. As she pedaled on, she prayed that she would not be followed beyond the bounds of Salzevar. Fortunately for her, the turbaned youths became involved with a rival gang, and turned upon them with their fusillade of stones, so she managed to escape before she received any worse injuries.

For the remainder of that day, in ever-increasing pain, she continued to pedal along the rough track. It proved to be treacherous going, for on the occasional smooth stretches thin sand blown off the desert had produced a surface on which she frequently skidded. First the hostility of the people of Salzevar, now this dangerous surface. She was tempted to wonder whether Fate had turned against her enterprise. But she ended that day in the police barracks of a small but apparently friendly village. By now she was feeling ill, and strongly suspected that she was running a feverish temperature. She had not brought a thermometer with her, so could only guess what that temperature might be.

To her immense relief, she woke next morning without a trace of the fever and in general feeling much better than she had when she arrived at Bagh-Jar police barracks. Her right arm, however, still worried her a good deal. By now it was half as large again as her left arm, and it was obvious that at any moment the blisters not already punctured by the stone throwing would burst. They spread almost the full length of her arm, from shoulder to wrist, and were a very ugly sight indeed. But for the time being at least there was absolutely nothing she could do about them, save treat them with some of the soothing medicated cream she carried with her as soon as they burst.

Her day's mileage fell badly that day, though she did manage to cover more than fifty in all—a pretty good performance in view of the state of the track she was following. Of those fifty miles she had to walk twelve, and practically carry her heavily loaded cycle. But the splendor and drama of the mountain scenery into which the track now brought her were so impressive that she covered those long miles almost with a sense of exaltation.

The latter part of her day's trek was easier, for now the track descended to the foothills and thence to more desert, and this lasted until she reached the little town of Nishapur. Here she had a totally unexpected and very pleasant encounter with one of the villagers. She was, as she said afterward, "captured" by a student and became his parents' guest for the night. The youth quickly showed that what he was chiefly interested in was opportunity to practice speaking English. He told her that this was the language that all Persians wanted to master. Incidentally, he pointed out to her that she was in the "Omar Khayyam Country," and she had hardly had time to wash before she was whisked away by the student and a group of his close friends to visit Omar Khayyam's tomb, recently opened officially to the public.

This was Dervla Murphy's first encounter with Persians, other than the authorities in Tehran and the various local police in whose barracks she stayed overnight. It gave her much to think about when she went on her way the following morning. The mother of the family was only a few years older than herself, thirty-five, in fact. But she had a family of three sons, the oldest of whom was twenty, and four daughters ranging from sixteen years old to six.

So important did the family consider the advent of their unexpected guest that they rounded up every relative they had in the district. There were no fewer than twelve of these. She noticed that even though they were close relatives, mother and daughters alike, including the six-year-old, veiled themselves completely before the menfolk entered their home. By Muslim law, she was told, it was forbidden for any but husband and sons to catch even a glimpse of a woman's countenance.

Heartened by the unexpected and generous hospitality, and the change of diet, in which lentils for once took the place of the rice on which she seemed to have subsisted all too long, and a savory omelette and a salad were followed by a dessert of some sugary substance which she could not identify but certainly enjoyed, she set off in good spirits to cover the seventy-odd miles to her next stopping-place, Sang Bast. The road was easier than it had been for some time, and there was much less climbing to do. On the other hand, the wind had shifted overnight to the east, so she had to pedal hard and steadily, whatever the surface, to make any headway at all. As she pedaled, there still echoed in her ears the strange Persian music she had listened to throughout the long evening in the student's crowded home. It had been music for dancing, played on a timbrel by one of the girls of the household while most of the others, including the six-year-old, danced for hours on end and the mother and grandmother smoked a hookah turn and turn about and looked on indulgently as the younger folk enjoyed themselves.

She stopped for a rest in the middle of the day and exchanged bread and salt with a villainous looking but friendly Persian shepherd. He gave her to understand, by pointing at the sky and making fluttering movements with his fingers, that they could expect rain within the next day or two. Before leaving Tehran, a week earlier, she had been told that South Persia had quite recently had its first inch of rain in four days.

Now she was within a day or two's ride of the frontier between Persia and Afghanistan, when another major "milestone" would have been successfully passed. Feeling that she had little time to spare, she branched off the road she had been following in the general direction of Herat, and thence to Kabul, to have a look at the town of Meshed. She had arranged to pick up mail from home there, and also spare gear both for herself and for her machine. These should be awaiting her at the British Consulate. In fact, she had hardly set foot in Meshed when, as the friendly shepherd had foretold, it began to rain.

Her first impression was not a happy one. She encountered a number of men and youths wearing the same sort of turban as those who had stoned her in Salzevar. She wisely made straight for the Consulate. There she was casually informed that only a day or two before an American girl had imprudently wandered off by herself for an hour, to take photographs of the minarets, and had been set upon and badly injured with stones by these same roving gangs. They were known as Mullahs, and claimed to be directly descended from the Prophet himself.

During the conversation, everything seemed to point to the wisdom of the authorities in Tehran who had tried their best to dissuade her from continuing her solo journey, and to her folly in challenging their advice. Three Americans, she was told, had been set upon by bandits not far short of the Afghan frontier, and shot dead. The bandits made their escape across the frontier, but the Afghan police chased them back across their own frontier. Meanwhile the Persian authorities had been alerted, troops were sent out from Tehran to comb the mountainous borderland and bring them to justice. The men had been captured, brought to Tehran, and there publicly hanged. This was intended, of course, as a warning to the other bandits known to infest this wild border country, but it was too soon, as yet, to know if the warning had been effective. The speaker added that the route over which this lone cyclist planned to continue her journey eastward lay through this borderland. Though he did not give it in so many words, his message was plain enough.

Meshed was the last town for some while where there was any prospect of repairs to Roz. Undaunted by the warnings she had received, Dervla Murphy went off into the back streets to try to locate a bicycle shop. She knew there would be one, for bicycles exist in Persia in enormous numbers, though usually in a terrible state of dilapidation. She soon found the sort of place she was looking for, but she had yet to learn that Persian mechanics are what might be called "hammer-and-chisel men." They never, it seemed, screw a screw into its hole, but prefer to bash it home with a heavy hammer, regardless of its delicate thread. She sat on a stool and watched a so-called mechanic assail her beloved Roz as though he was filled with hatred for the machine and determined to destroy it completely. In horror at what he was doing, she quickly gave the man some coins and snatched Roz from him. Once on the road, she threw her leg over the saddle and set off southeastward without looking back, to chance her luck once more.

Once again she was obliged to break her rule about not traveling after dark, for it was dusk when she left Meshed and she had some miles to go before reaching Sang Bast, where she had spent the previous night. About twelve miles, she reckoned, in all. But since she had already covered this length of branch road once, she did not anticipate any trouble when returning over it. She was very, very wrong.

Part way between Meshed and Sang Bast a car with five men inside it slowed down alongside her and brought her to an awkward halt. One of the occupants leaned out and invited her to join them. She refused, and attempted to continue on her way. The man became pressing. A car door was opened, and it was made quite clear to her that what she was expected to do was to abandon her cycle and become a passenger—one woman among five strange and, as it seemed to her by then, pretty sinister-looking men. She noticed that one of them had a rifle, and was fingering it, meaningfully.

Were they, she speculated desperately, a special type of bandit that operated by car instead of lurking among the mountain defiles to attack the wayfarer? Or were they, perhaps, quite friendly and well-disposed toward her, genuinely anxious to see her to her destination in safety? She could not be sure of the answer to her questions, but her strong instinct was to distrust them entirely. True, she carried a lightweight pistol, but she had sense enough to know that to threaten men like these, in lawless country like this, with its wild traditions, would be more likely to spark off retaliation than to strike fear into their hearts.

As she hesitated, she heard the unmistakable clip-clop of a horse's hoofs. She looked toward the sound. In the light of the car's one headlamp she saw a policeman approaching. The car's driver saw him at the same moment. Any suspicions she might have had were now promptly confirmed. For the driver raced his engine, let in his clutch with a bang, and the car took a leap forward that left her covered with grit and dust, and half choked with exhaust fumes.

The policeman dismounted, and she recognized him as quickly as he recognized her—he was one of the squad of men who occupied the Sang Bast barracks. She could not follow in detail what he now said to her, but the general drift of what he said was clear enough. She was to mount, and continue on her way. As for him, he would remain within easy reach all the time. And as for them—he shook his fist in the direction the car had taken. Probably he knew who the occupants were, and they would doubtless be making themselves as scarce as possible and with the least possible delay.

An hour later Dervla Murphy was safely back in the police barracks. One of the men noticed her badly blistered arm, and registered extreme concern. He routed about on a shelf and produced a tube of cream. He unscrewed the top, and applied some of its contents to the largest of the burst blisters. She flinched—not so much at the anticipated pain as at the thought of what else the tube might have been used for. Did it contain some local product that might do her skin more harm than good? Then, in the dim light of the room she fancied she spotted the words "Made in Switzerland." For the second time in little more than an hour she heaved a deep sigh of relief.

She was now only about one hundred miles from Ghurion, a township on the Persian-Afghan border. She made as early a start as possible the next morning, and was actually in the saddle soon after five o'clock. Only one thing marred the pleasantness of her overnight stop in the police barracks where one of the men had been so concerned about her blistered arm. When she was packing her things in readiness to leave, she found that sixty American cigarettes had been taken from one of the baskets. Obviously the culprit must be one of the men, but she did not feel that she was in a position to charge them with theft. The temptation to steal must have been great, for cigarettes of that quality were a rare luxury in Persia. As she said goodbye to them, she looked at each of them in turn. Not one of them so much as batted an eyelid. She thanked them for their hospitality. From the doorway, they watched her leave. She was generous enough to hope that they would all enjoy a good smoke for as long as the stolen booty lasted.

Cycling briskly, over a stretch of road very much better than many over which she had alternately cycled and walked, she had covered forty miles by the middle of the morning. Then, disaster befell her: Roz's rear wheel came adrift between the forks. Luckily she was pedaling slowly up a gentle incline when this happened. Had she been coasting downhill there might have been a very nasty accident. As it was, her machine simply stopped beneath her. She was not surprised. After the ferocious battering it had received at the Meshed mechanic's hands it was really remarkable that it had lasted as long as this. Supposing, too, that this had happened to her on the way back to Sang Bast, in the dark! She might have been obliged to accept a lift from the men in the car that had appeared so suddenly and departed so speedily when the mounted policeman appeared.

She realized that this time she was in dire trouble. The last place she had passed through lay some twenty-five miles behind her; the next place of any size lay twenty miles ahead of her. To continue her journey on foot was clearly impossible, for now her machine could not even be wheeled, and certainly she could not carry it. She was, then, completely stranded.

Philosophically, she made herself as comfortable as she could by the roadside and settled down to wait until either a truck or a bus or some other vehicle hove into view, going in the right direction. She had not seen a single vehicle all that morning, but she was an optimist at heart, and told herself firmly, as the sun rose higher and higher overhead and the temperature rose with it to more than a hundred degrees, that since nothing had come her way in the past six hours, something was bound to do so before so very long.

Early in the afternoon she dropped off into a doze. She was wakened from it by the roar and rumble of a truck coming up the road. It was the first that day, and a chance not to be missed. It came to a staggering halt, and an Afghan with a flowing turban leaned out of the cab as she went over to him. He did not need to be told what she required. Without a word, he snatched up her mutilated bicycle and piled it onto the mixed cargo already stacked precariously on his vehicle. As he roped it down, he noticed her blistered arm, and its impact on him was surprising.

Still without a word, he reached into a tin beneath the dashboard and extracted a handful of gray cotton. He dipped this into some grease in a tin marked "Premium Pure Motor Oil" and smeared the whole length of her arm with it. In spite of her instinctive horror at what he was doing, she found his touch extraordinarily gentle, and as precise as that of any nurse. She told herself that however dirty the cotton might be, and however improbable the motor oil was as an ointment, she could hardly be in a worse state than she was already. The Afghan completed his ministrations, flashed a brilliant smile at her and let in the clutch with his bare foot. The truck lurched off, roaring and whining, and was soon once again in full stride.

The track on which she had been cycling until disaster befell her had seemed bad. Now, perched on the floor of the truck's cab, while the driver himself balanced on an upturned crate, for there was neither passenger nor driver's seat in this relic of a vehicle, it seemed to her that there was no track at all. Like all the drivers she had seen so far, he was driving bare-footed with complete unconcern. The crazily-built truck, whose cab had no windshield, no side-window and no doors, lurched from side to side like a ship in a storm. Fumes poured from the engine, which of course had no hood to cover it, and streamed into the cab through the non-existent windshield so that she was permanently enveloped in a blue haze. She began to feel sick, and wondered whether she would have to ask the Afghan to stop so that she could make a dash for the side of the road and be sick there, instead of actually in the cab.

Luckily, for her at any rate, just when things had become desperate, the truck was brought to a screeching and grinding halt—one of the tires had blown. Dervla Murphy took this welcome opportunity to walk up and down the side of the track, inhaling as much fresh air as she could before the nightmare journey had to be resumed. Nearly a hundred miles, she had gathered from the driver, lay ahead of them before they would came to a town where her bicycle could be properly repaired. It was a small town named Tieabad.

A hundred miles of this sort of travel! She blanched at the prospect. But walking alongside the track had shown her that even if her bicycle had been in first-class condition she would probably have been unable to ride it except for a few hundred yards at a time, for it was now as bad as anything she had seen until then. So, probably, she would have been reduced anyway to thumbing a lift from a truck, a thing which she regarded always as a last resort.

They set off again. The fumes from the engine seemed to be worse than ever. She wondered whether she might actually pass out as a result of having to inhale them. People, after all, had been known to die from exhaust poisoning. She comforted herself with the thought that the Afghan driver, at any rate, did not seem to be suffering any ill effects!

Again fortunately (for her at least), the truck broke down. And yet again. Each time it was something different. It was as though Fate was intervening on her behalf. Each time she reached the point where she felt that she could not stand it another minute, something brought the truck to an abrupt standstill. There was another puncture. There was a choked gas pipe. Something fell off the back of the truck, and hearing it (astonishingly) above the roar of his engine, the Afghan had to bring the thing to a standstill and then walk back along the track to collect it and wedge it into position among the rest of his miscellaneous load.

It seemed an eternity before they rolled into the outskirts of Tieabad. Dervla Murphy took some comfort from the fact that her blistered arm felt no worse than it had before the truck journey began. So, even if there had been dirt in the cotton and unknown ingredients in the motor oil with which her arm had been so liberally smeared, no foreign body, apparently, had seeped into her bloodstream! Thanks to the lift, she was a full day and more ahead of her schedule. She would get her bicycle repaired and then push on under her own steam, to complete the journey to the Afghan frontier. If the truck driver was a sample of what the natives of

Afghanistan were like, then she might expect a happy and rewarding stage of her long journey once she had reached the other side of the frontier. His never-failing smile lingered in her memory long after he had gone on his way.

In Tieabad she found, as he had said she would, a back-street bicycle-repair shop. Remembering her unhappy experience in Meshed, she was cautious about allowing this mechanic to operate on Roz without close supervision. Certainly he gave the appearance of being another hammer-and-chisel man, but this time she was prepared. At the risk of offending him by indicating that she was something of a handyman herself, she went through his scanty stock of nuts and bolts until she found what looked like the items she required. Then, deliberately seizing a spanner from his makeshift bench, and showing him what she wanted done, she practically "willed" him into making the necessary repair to the rear forks.

She recognized the fact that she might well be wounding his pride, but the matter was more than just one of pride, so far as she was concerned: she had to get Roz in order for a long and exacting stage of her marathon journey, and so could not afford to give way to mere sentiment. Luckily for her the man seemed friendly. Between them they completed the repair. She paid him—probably a good deal more than he would have got from any local bicycle owner who had come in for a repair to his machine—and they parted on friendly terms.

She spent the night in Tieabad, but was astride her machine early the next morning. It was six o'clock, and she had just nineteen more Persian miles to do before finding herself at the Afghan Customs Post on the outskirts of Ghurion. Desert stretched far into the distance on either side of the track. Sand had been blown across it to such an extent that she had to guess very often where the track was to be found. The blown sand was thick enough to fill up the cracks and holes, and as before it was loose enough to present a curiously skiddy surface. More than once this brought her off her machine. In spite of this, she covered the nineteen miles in an hour and three quarters.

About halfway along those nineteen miles she came unexpectedly on a huge stone pillar that stood more than seven feet high. It bore on its face the single word: Afghanistan. She stopped just long enough to take a photograph of Roz with the rear wheel in Persia and the front wheel in Afghanistan, and then rode on. A couple of miles further on was an advance Customs Post. It consisted of nothing more than a tree branch laid across the track. A very young soldier, hardly more than a boy by his looks, lay close to one end of the branch, sound asleep. Unwilling to interrupt his slumbers, she delicately negotiated the obstacle, and continued on her way to the real Customs Post some distance ahead.

Of all the Customs Posts she had passed through, or was later to pass through, this proved to be the most informal, the officials the most courteous. They offered her tea, invited her to make herself comfortable in a darkened room, did everything in their power to make her welcome. The three men, in baggy cotton trousers and long embroidered garments resembling old-fashioned nightshirts, sat with her on a carpet, crosslegged, and contrived to talk with her even though they did not speak a single word of English. And, so far as the actual words used by them were concerned, every one of them was completely new to her. But there was friendliness in the very air of that room, and she felt herself blossoming, forgetting the hardships and anxieties and very real dangers that had attended the last many miles of her eastward journey through Persia to the Afghan frontier.

The men did, however, try very hard indeed—as the authorities at Tehran had done a week and more ago—to dissuade her from continuing along the road into Afghanistan. By signs and gestures they made it quite clear to her that the road conditions would be very much worse than anything she had experienced up till then. She doubted whether in fact this was possible. And she made it equally clear that she was determined to continue eastward on her bicycle, in spite of their friendly but emphatic warnings.

Then one of the three men had what seemed to him a bright idea. His main concern all along, it seemed, had been that in the desert-like territory through which she would now have to travel for many miles there was no water. As a result, she would almost certainly suffer dreadfully, as other travelers before her had, from dehydration. She might even die—as others before her had done. But, he went on more cheerfully, since she was so resolute to complete her journey on her bicycle, there was a solution to the problem. At any moment now they could expect the arrival of one of the scheduled gas-delivery trucks, eastward bound from a depot beyond Meshed and with Herat, in Afghanistan, as its destination. When, as he was bound to do, he stopped at this frontier Customs Post to have his papers checked, the driver would be given two cans of drinking water. He would be instructed to dump these by the roadside, the first of them fifteen miles beyond the frontier, and the second one after another thirty miles.

So, much heartened by her reception, the lone cyclist departed on the next stage of her journey. As she cycled away from the frontier Customs Post she thought of the good fellowship and the kindly consideration for her welfare that she had received at the officials' hands. It was a good omen for the stages she would have to cover in this new land. She was comforted, in this area of desert land, by the prospect of finding at convenient intervals along her route drinking water dumped for her use as a result of the thoughtfulness of the men with whom she had sat drinking tea in the cool dimness of their lonely Customs Post. The township of Ghurion was her next objective. There she would begin the next major stage of her long solo journey which was to end, if she was to fulfil her self-imposed aim, at Delhi itself.

Dervla Murphy started riding through Afghanistan on April 10th. She reached Delhi almost exactly three months later, in the second week of July. She had fulfilled a dream that had been with her since she had been a small girl some twenty years before.

John Hillaby in Search of Lake Rudolf

In the early 1960s a young man with a passion for long-distance walking decided that he would like to trek through mountain and desert territory in northwest Kenya in search of a lake that lies close to the Uganda border, with its northern tip on the frontier of Kenya and Ethiopia. It would be a journey of some eleven hundred miles out and back, a journey that very few men had made since the lake was discovered in 1888 by an Austrian traveler, Count Teleki von Szek. He named this great and lonely stretch of water after Crown Prince Rudolf of Austria, though it has also become known as "The Jade Sea."

Count Teleki made his journey as explorers did in his day. He was accompanied by no fewer than six guides, three Swahilis, eight Somalis, fifteen "askaris," or African trained soldiers, and two hundred native carriers. The expedition planned by young John Hillaby was on a much more modest scale. He enlisted the services of four camel men who knew much of the region, and he had six camels for baggage and riding and general duties.

Hillaby had had no experience of desert or bush conditions. He knew only a few words of the language spoken by the natives and he had never so much as seen a camel, except in the zoo. He had never in his life handled any sort of gun. But he was athletically built and immensely fit, and possessed great stamina and powers of endurance. Possibly his greatest asset lay in the fact that he had a keen sense of humor and was a born optimist. His three-month safari was going to demonstrate the need for all these qualities, and for others besides.

Only a very large scale map of Kenya would indicate John Hillaby's actual starting-point, for it was not a town, but consisted of what is known locally as a *boma,* or kraal—a small collection of native huts—named Wamba. The kraal is to be found some eighty miles to the north of Mt. Kenya. He left this kraal on December 6, 1962, and reached his objective just thirteen days later, on December 19th.

The route that he planned lay roughly northward, diverging sometimes to the northeast, sometimes to the northwest, according to the general lie of the land, the steepness of the hills to be climbed and the desert terrain that had to be crossed. He had no illusions as to the challenges he would have to face if he was to complete his trek in search of this lake, which very few white men had ever seen in the seventy-odd years since its discovery, and return safely to his Kenya base. He had read and re-read the account written by Teleki's Austrian companion during the 1888 safari, and knew almost by heart a paragraph that ran as follows:

> The mountain district between us and the lake was a veritable Hell, consisting of a series of parallel heights running from north to south which we had to cut across in a north-westerly fashion. The slopes of the mountains were steep precipices, most of them quite insurmountable, and those that were not, were strewn with blackish-brown blocks of rock or loose "scoriae." The narrow valleys were encumbered with stones or débris, or with deep loose sand in which our feet sank, making progress difficult. And when the sun rose higher, its rays were reflected from the smooth, brownish-black surface of the rock, causing an almost intolerable glare, whilst a burning wind from the south whirled the sand in our faces and almost blew the loads off the heads of the native carriers.

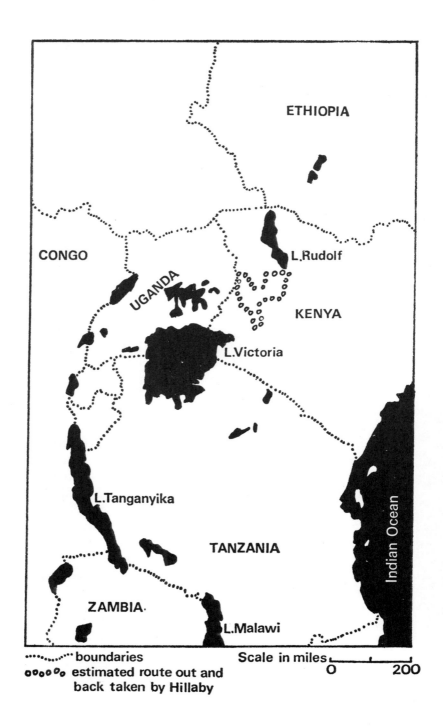

In spite of this advance knowledge of the conditions that awaited him, John Hillaby set off on his trek in high spirits. On the advice of a better-known desert traveler, Wilfred P. Thesiger, he walked in lightweight rubber-and-canvas shoes, rather than in the heavy boots that are the accepted footwear for most travelers doing their journey the hard way. Such shoes, Thesiger had insisted, were far better than bush-boots for desert walking. They were lighter than boots by a great deal, and yet protected the feet. They were expendable. Hillaby stocked up on a dozen pairs, wore them time and time again, and discarded each pair as the soles wore through. He never regretted having taken Thesiger's unexpected advice.

In the early stages, the track alternated between a winding path at the bottom of a defile and a scramble over loose scree. On either side were poised great lumps of the brownish-black rock that Teleki had commented upon so often. They were sinister in color and shape, and as he was soon to find out for himself, often so loosely poised that the slightest stumble on the part of a man or a camel could dislodge them and send them leaping and bouncing down the steep slopes. There were baboons, unseen but very audible, higher up those hillsides, their cries strangely unnerving. From time to time, as he looked up into the burning dome of the sky, he saw an eagle hanging motionless, its vast wings outspread, as though awaiting its chance to swoop down on his little party trapped in the narrow defile and climbing so slowly toward the gap ahead of them through which—if they ever reached it—they would eventually emerge into yet another stretch of this hard and challenging territory.

When at last they reached the gap there was the long downward slope, over loose rubble, to negotiate. Hillaby recorded that looking northward he felt as though he was surveying the very edge of the known world. For untold miles to the horizon there extended a boundless stretch of sand and lava debris, a reminder (as if he needed it!) that the terrain to which he was now committed had once been volcanic. It was down onto that inhospitable-looking terrain that, somehow, he and his men and camels, all of them heavily laden with baggage, provisions and that most vital of all commodities in desert conditions, water, had to make their way.

The descent immediately revealed that it was going to be very much more arduous, and dangerous too, than the ascent had been. The track had been almost completely obliterated by a landslide, apparently recent. A massive collapse of hundreds of thousands of tons of the brownish-black stone that had threatened them all the way through the defile had now done its worst. There simply was no track whatsoever.

Two of the camel men went ahead, each holding the head-rope of the leading camel of each group of three, in an attempt to guide them over the least difficult portions of the route. Camels' feet, of course, are designed for walking on sand. Now, however, they were having to plant their feet on loose boulders, on jagged fragments of broken rock, and in the crevices between them. In these crevices their cushioned feet jammed as they drove their long, ungainly legs clumsily down beneath their heavy loads. Time and again the whole camel-train was brought to a halt and the men had to set to work to extricate a jammed hoof from a wedge-shaped crevice by sheer brute force, an operation that was accompanied by a continuous high-pitched volley of screams which Hillaby found almost unbearable.

Though curiously graceful when striding across open desert, the camels proved as ill-fitted for terrain such as this as a bicycle would have been. They pitched and tossed and collapsed with their legs sprawling at such wide angles that it seemed certain that they must have broken, or would break when they were being extricated. Every possible device—some of them, Hillaby thought, cruel in the extreme—was brought into use by the camel men in their efforts to persuade their beasts to help themselves. But the camel is as obstinate as a mule, and in some respects a good deal harder to handle. As the hours went by beneath the fierce sun, the men became more and more impatient in their repeated efforts to free their camels and get them in motion again.

One camel broke through an apparently safe bridge of slabs that the men had prepared for it, and fell into a cavity larger than any so far encountered. Its heavy load, secured by lengths of coarse rope to the V-shaped wooden framework lashed to its sides, checked it from falling right to the bottom. For a while the beast hung, suspended by its own load, its long, angular, ungainly legs lashing out unseen beneath it. The drivers knew that if the load ropes broke the camel would drop to the bottom of the cavity and nothing they could then do would extricate it this time. It looked as though it was doomed. The men discussed whether it would be better to remove its load and distribute this among the remaining camels, leaving this one to die where it had fallen. Hillaby wondered whether he would have to get out his gun and deliberately shoot it, to put it out of its misery. The prospect appalled him.

But the camel men were not yet beaten. It was evident, this time at any rate, that the usual routine, which consisted of beating the animal, twisting its tail, kicking its flanks and at the same time jerking on its headrope, the noose meanwhile wound tightly about its jaws to prevent it from biting, just would not have any effect at all. So, at considerable risk to themselves, two of them climbed down into the cavity and got beneath the camel's breastbone. Applying their shoulders to this, they heaved with all their might. The camel's legs flailed wildly, and at last found a ledge on which to press. Then, with the other men hauling from above, and all of them crying out slogans of encouragement, the two men below, operating like a pair of human hydraulic jacks, succeeded in levering the camel upward. A moment or two later, to everyone's surprise and delight, the camel had struggled clear of the cavity and was standing, trembling in all four legs, on comparatively safe ground. Froth poured from its flared nostrils as thick as soapsuds on wash day.

Though there had been a number of occasions when they had doubted whether they would ever succeed in doing so, they eventually got all six camels down from the landslide area onto relatively level ground at the bottom. Now, of course, they would have liked to make up for so much lost time. But the camel men knew, even if Hillaby did not, that a camel has its own set speed, and can rarely if ever be made to increase that speed. This, of course, refers to the traditional "ship-of-the-desert" type of camel, the traditional load-carrier. It is of a completely different breed from the famous racing camels so highly prized by their Arab owners. So, they plodded on, over near-level terrain sprinkled with scrub that had thorns capable of tearing skin and flesh to ribbons. Hillaby writes of a native who had apparently fallen foul of one of these vicious bushes. He gave the impression of having been flogged with a cat-o'-nine-tails manufactured from barbed wire.

In good time before darkness would begin to close in they looked for a suitable site to pitch camp. They had reached a stretch of open country in which acacias and prickly scrub grew in abundance, and this seemed to offer a reasonable promise of security from night prowlers. Hillaby took the precaution of indicating where he would locate his own tent. It would be up-wind of the camels, whose smell during the night was something that the camel drivers could endure more easily than he could, as he was not yet accustomed to such company.

The site did not prove to be a good one. A straying camel thrust a foot deep into a hole in the sand. Immediately there emerged a huge column of enormous black ants. As though to support them, and fearing a threat of danger to their community, two other columns of these monster ants streamed out from holes close by, and converged with military precision on the first. Then two more similar columns appeared, and in all there were now five columns of giant marching ants, two yards and more in length and eighteen inches or so wide, with the outsize, big-jawed "soldier" ants flanking them. Experts say that these are probably the most viciously dangerous creatures in the whole African continent. A tethered horse has been known to be stripped to its skeleton by such armies of ants. Their capacity for flesh rivals that of the deadly Brazilian piranha, even though they are so very much smaller than those river fish.

Hillaby was told an interesting story about these black ants, which shows how imagination and original thinking can sometimes turn even such horrors to good use. A hunter on the lower slopes of the Ruwenzori, known also as the Mountains of the Moon, was attacked by a leopard, which tore off a huge strip of skin and flesh from his side. He knew that without prompt help he would probably bleed to death, but he was very far indeed from any possible medical assistance. The resourceful hunter therefore looked about him until he came on a swarm of these soldier ants. He picked up a number of them, one at a time, and deliberately set each in turn on the line where the flesh had been torn away. The ant embedded its powerful jaws in the flesh. The hunter then cut away the body, so that the jaws remained immovable in his own flesh. Soon he had a long line of these "stitches," composed of ants' jaws. The blood ceased to flow from his wound, and he was able to return to his base and receive proper medical treatment instead of slowly bleeding to death there on the lonely mountainside.

Not surprisingly, the camel men insisted that they must look for an alternative camp site. They knew that they and their beasts would be at a hopeless disadvantage if they had to share it with so many others, even though they were so small. They moved on, and came at length to another site.

There they settled down. A welcome meal was prepared, and soon afterward they all turned in for the night. They all knew that the following day's march was likely to prove every bit as arduous as the one they had just completed.

The next morning they faced, for the first but by no means the last time, a problem that took a good deal of solving. At frequent intervals they found themselves confronted by "luggas," or dried-up stream beds. Certainly the terrain they were crossing did not look as though it had ever been well watered. Generally it was as arid as any named desert, though it had more tumbled rocks and boulders than true sand dunes. But obviously there must at some time have been watercourses crisscrossing this region in the far northwest of Kenya—the existence of these luggas proved it. But they were a true menace to progress. They were steeply banked on both sides, and the bottom was a tumbled mass of loose stones and rubble. To persuade the camels to go down one side and up the other was an almost insuperable task, and it was one that had to be continually undertaken.

The task at the very first of these crossings was aggravated by the fact that a herd of what appeared to be *red* elephants had apparently selected it as a meeting-place. If there is one beast that invariably terrifies a camel, it is an elephant —whether red or otherwise. The brick-red appearance of these particular elephants was due to the fact that they were indulging in the common practice among elephants of dusting themselves with whatever lay readiest at hand. In this case it was the reddish-brown sandy soil that filled the spaces between the boulders in the bottom of the lugga.

This one was as deep and wide as a railway cutting. The only points along the sides which were reasonably graded for descent and ascent seemed to have been used by the elephants themselves, who then remained at the bottom of the slide they had created, to relax and dust themselves. Several hours were lost by the small party in their search along the near side for a point at which they could hope to make their way safely down into the deep, stony channel and then up out of it again.

Eventually they found one. With much labor and ingenuity—not all of it approved by Hillaby, though he was wise enough not to interfere—the apprehensive camels, linked by their headropes, were induced to slither down into the stony bed. There was much screaming, which was audible high above the shouts and oaths of the exasperated camel men. But the position was not much better when they were down in the lugga, for the opposite side proved on closer inspection to be quite impossible to climb. The only alternative was to continue northeastward along the dried-up riverbed until they came to a breach in the opposite bank which the camels could be induced to climb.

The going was extremely hard. The stones and small boulders were packed around with loose, red, sandy soil. Into this, the men's feet penetrated until often they were knee, or even thigh deep. The camels negotiated the soft sandy soil more successfully, but they continually tripped over the half-submerged boulders. From time to time one of them would collapse beneath its load and lie spreadeagled, its long neck lying out ahead of it like the bowsprit of a foundering yacht. It then took the combined efforts of all the camel men and Hillaby too to persuade it to stagger to its feet again.

Then, without warning, an elephant appeared on top of the bank, silhouetted menacingly against the blazing empiness of the sky. The leading camel became aware of it, and took fright instantly. So violent was its reaction that it snapped the length of rope, not between itself and the second camel in the string of three, but between the second and the third. Released from this anchorage, the two leading camels stampeded, edging their way up the near bank and continually slipping on the slope and plunging dangerously down again, with the permanent risk of breaking their legs. Their panic affected the others, and within minutes all six camels were rioting. They darted away, jerking from one side to the other so violently that one or two of them broke the ropes that attached their loads to the carrier-frames and so jettisoned them to the ground. The camels screamed, the men yelled as they raced after them, tripping and stumbling as they ran. Hillaby began to wonder whether his trek was coming to an end long before they came in sight of its objective.

At last some measure of calm was restored. The big elephant that had been responsible for the panic stood motionless for a while. Then, as though puzzled by what it had witnessed down below, it wandered off in the opposite direction, shaking its massive head from one side to the other, in search perhaps of its fellows. The party was reassembled, though only with the utmost difficulty, and at long last came to a point where it proved possible to climb out of the lugga on the far side. It had taken many hours of sustained and exhausting labor to unite the camels, rope them up again, and collect the items of equipment and stores that had been jettisoned while the panic was on. Hillaby wisely decided to call a halt earlier than usual that day. They found a site free of ants and other pests, pitched their tents, gathered scrub wood for a campfire, and settled down to a meal before going to sleep.

That evening, Hillaby took stock of what had been lost as a result of the panic that had swept through the camel train. A valuable stove had vanished, and with it its fuel. One of their lamps had been smashed beyond repair, though it had been salvaged. His shaving-mirror was splintered. A number of bottles had been broken, and their precious contents spilled to the ground. Half a sack of maize had been lost, and a sack of rice as well. More important, perhaps, a chest containing water-purifying equipment appeared to have been spirited away, like the stove. No one had seen it go, no one knew where it was. For a moment, Hillaby considered working his way back along the lugga in search of it, but this proposal, he reflected, might well lead to mutiny. He must simply cut his losses and trust to Providence that none of the water they used when their present supplies ran out would be so bad that purification was essential if they were not all to be poisoned by it.

It was as they sat around their campfire a few days later that he first heard mention of what his camel men referred to as the "upepo." They spoke of it as a great wind that blew off the Kulal and other mountains on the route to Lake Rudolf and was so fierce that no man could withstand it. When it blew, as it so often did, across wasteland and desert, it carried clouds of sand with it that could engulf whole encampments and bring about death by sheer suffocation. Was this exaggeration, he wondered. Certainly their stories reminded him of the writings of an earlier traveler in these parts. Had not Teleki's companion recorded that the winds were so strong that they almost blew the loads off the heads of their native bearers? Well, only time would tell whether these stories were true or not.

By mid-morning of the next day the heat had become almost unendurable. The terrain they were approaching shimmered in the heat as though its surface was alive and somehow on the move. Even the slopes of the hills ahead quivered under its impact. Beneath their feet was ancient, broken lava. Walking on it in his lightweight shoes, Hillaby felt that it was almost molten beneath the thin soles. And the heat increased hour by hour, almost minute by minute. There was no shade whatsoever, except that beneath the bellies of their camels. Except for the fact that the terrain lacked the harsh shadows now known to exist on the surface of the moon, it might have been a lunar landscape across which this small party of men and beasts was doomed to march. It seemed a curiously dead sort of world, and one in which they were the only living objects.

Here and there a lugga crossed the line of their route, and had therefore to be negotiated, since it could never be bypassed. They never met one as difficult as the one that had been adopted by the red elephants, the one that actually bore a name on the map—Milgris. But each successive dried-up watercourse called for care and strength and determination in its crossing, and not one of them rewarded them with so much as a trickle of water in return. This shortage of water had become a very real threat. They now had only a bare four gallons in hand. One of the camel men assured Hillaby that there was a good waterhole not far ahead of them. But by then Hillaby had learned that in the language of the camel men "not far" could mean almost anything; and "good water," by their standards, might well not be drinkable at all by Western standards.

Now their track began to climb again. The ascent, though not very steep, added considerably to the efforts entailed by marching. The lava flow was generally smooth, but it was continuously interrupted by blocks of the dark stone of which Teleki's companion had written. It resembled coarse slag, and was very hard on the feet, often tearing off the homemade sandals the camel men wore, which they had manufactured from strips of old rubber tires lashed to their naked feet with thongs of rope. There was that other emanation from volcanoes, too—pumice-stone. It reminded Hillaby of cheese. Though comparatively soft, it proved as hot to the touch as the lava itself.

There was now a little wind. True, it was no more than an idle stirring of the hot air. He felt as though he was walking past an interminable series of open oven doors, from which wafts of super-heated air emanated. Surely this cannot be the dreaded upepo, he thought. But after an hour or two of this, he began to be conscious of a distant moaning sound from somewhere in the direction of Kulal, the mountain always associated with the upepo. The vague sound rose in tone to something more resembling a distant screaming. It was not so strident as that produced by the camels when in pain or fear, but it reminded him of this.

It came rapidly closer. Whereas a few moments before it had seemed remote, now it impinged on his eardrums. And with the sound came the phenomenon familiar to all those who have ever set foot in the desert: the so-called "dust devils." These are scurrying, windborne miniature pillars of sand that race across the surface, spinning, whirling, spiraling as they go, in such a strange fashion that it is easy to see why they have acquired this nickname. Sometimes they come in "single spies," sometimes in "battalions."

The camel men took action without further delay. Headropes were checked and, where necessary, tightened. Used as camels are to desert conditions, they cannot be relied on not to take flight in a sandstorm. Now, as though all of one mind, the six camels began to slant off the route, away from the increasing strength of the wind and the sand that it carried so viciously in its teeth. They had to be continually and violently wrenched back onto course. But when it became evident that the party would soon have to face up to a real storm, the leading camel man promptly made for the first depression he could find in the lava surface over which they were staggering, and called an emphatic halt.

Into the small depression they all wedged themselves, sheltering as best they could behind the bulk of their camels, which had now lowered themselves to the ground, and as their unpleasant custom is, were belching away one after another. Hillaby noticed, and not for the first time, that the camel men had a most unpleasant habit—to rid themselves of the fine sand that had accumulated in the folds of the skin of their weatherbeaten hands and even their faces, they now rinsed themselves with camels' urine.

The wind increased, and with it the clouds of sand. It was obvious that they would have to give up marching for that day, and settle down for the night in the hope that conditions would be better next morning. Hillaby asked that his tent should be set up. The head camel man warned him that if, as he anticipated, the upepo were to blow during the hours of darkness, the tent would be destroyed. He was somewhat brusquely told to do as he had been bidden. Grinning, he erected the tent, and Hillaby moved into it with relief, and proceeded to shroud himself with the mosquito netting he carried with him to ward off the pests that always attacked as soon as darkness had fallen over the desert.

He had not long been asleep when he was rudely wakened by the shriek as of an express train approaching. Before he had time to absorb the fact that this, at last, was the dreaded upepo advancing at full speed, his tent was whisked away from above him and he was left fully exposed to the wind and blown sand's fury save for his flimsy mosquito netting. This promptly followed the tent into the darkness, for he had taken it off, and failed to realize what the wind could do with it. They sheltered as best they could to the lee of the camels, and when it was light, had the prospect of salvaging tent and netting from the thornbushes on which they had become impaled. As might be expected, neither tent nor netting was ever the same again.

The morning dawned inauspiciously. The screaming of the upepo, Hillaby recorded, was of a "skull-wrinkling intensity." It was a blisteringly hot wind, too, once the sun was up. It whistled among the thornbushes, causing them to set up a peculiar high-pitched moan that had a disconcertingly human quality about it. Carried on the wind was sand. It had piled up against his tent, until this was whisked away. Now it was piling up around the men and their beasts too. If they stayed longer, they ran the risk of suffocation. The upepo, he was reminded, had been known to blow for as long as four days on end. Only the leader among the camel men thought there was any chance that the wind would die away in the afternoon.

They ate a breakfast that consisted of a handful of dates apiece and a mouthful or two of porridge oats slightly moistened from their precious supply of water. Sand seemed as plentiful as the flakes of oats, and the sticky dates were impregnated with it too. The meal occupied only a matter of minutes. While the men loaded the camels, Hillaby walked away and laboriously climbed a low hill in the hope of obtaining some idea of the sort of terrain they would have to cross when they made a start. It was not encouraging. There was an uneven surface of sand and rock rubble, scattered with gigantic boulders that had been picked up eons before by the lava flow and deposited at random. The boulders gave the curious impression of glistening in the sun. He discovered when he came closer to them that they had in fact been burnished by the abrasive action of windblown sand sweeping over them ever since they had been deposited there, when those remote volcanic disturbances had begun to create this nightmare landscape.

When he turned back toward the camp, the wind was so strong that he had to lean hard up against it to make any progress at all. It was reassuring to realize that the wind would not actually be against them when they started out northward again. And—did he only imagine it?—was the wind as strong as it had been when daylight broke? He thought not. And he remembered that his chief camel man had been unexpectedly optimistic about the duration of the upepo, though his fellow camel men had not agreed with him.

On the inadequate map Hillaby had obtained, and which of course he alone could read, there was an important northward-running track, named Sirima, which was said to lead almost directly to the southern end of Lake Rudolf. He knew that it was absolutely essential to locate this track. If they did not, they might wander indefinitely in this wasteland, even though he had a compass and knew how to use it. But the likelihood of actually striking this Sirima track seemed small. When they set out the sand was still being blown, as it had been for many hours past, from one side of the region to the other. It had obliterated their own footprints from the day before, and obliterated every vestige of a track such as the one they had been following and hoped to continue to follow. The foothills of Kulal and the Longippi ranges, that they had relied on as landmarks, were now almost completely hidden by orange-colored streamers of sand, borne on the wings of the upepo.

After setting out, they found themselves climbing steadily. The gradient was not severe, but it was aggravated by the innumerable boulders and fragmented rocks among which they had laboriously to pick their way. For a while it was as bad as anything they had experienced, with the possible exception of that cruel descent of the early range of hills when it seemed at every moment that they would lose their pack-animals even if they might hope to survive themselves.

The camel men were obviously very worried indeed by the haze that lay ahead of them. They knew well that it was not just a heat haze, but the outer edge of a more substantial sandstorm than any they had encountered so far. As they came nearer to it, Hillaby could see for himself the reason for their apprehension. There now seemed to be a moving mass of fine sand, carried on the wind and driving purposefully across the route to which they were committed. Oddly, it seemed to be channeled in one direction, for they themselves were marching over sand and rock only slightly affected, so far, by the windborne sand. But if they were to keep to this direction, the one likeliest to bring them to the Sirima track, then they would have to go right into this danger area.

The head camel man, whose opinions carried more weight than those of his fellows, urged Hillaby to halt before it was too late. If they camped now, he said, or at any rate very soon, there was a good chance that this major sandstorm would have blown itself out before they reached the area of the desert over which it was raging. He reminded his employer that the upepo could stop as suddenly as it started. This made good sense. But on the other hand there was the vital matter of thirst. The party was now down to its last can of water. There had been the promise of a good waterhole somewhere ahead of them. But to reach this and replenish their failing supply before it was too late, they would have to keep moving as fast as they could persuade their camels to move. But again, to do this would mean plunging right into the sandstorm ahead of them. Hillaby was debating the dilemma within himself when the decision was made for him. As one man, the camel drivers came to an abrupt halt, brought their beasts to their knees, and thus gave a clear indication of their intention to go no farther that day.

When at last they were able to move on, Hillaby had a better understanding of Teleki's report on this stage of their journey seventy and more years earlier. His companion had written:

> No living creature shared the solitude with us. As far as our glass could reach, there was nothing to be seen but desert, desert everywhere. To all this was added the scorching heat and the ceaseless buffeting of the sand-laden wind, against which we were powerless to protect ourselves.

Hillaby remembered something else besides. The Austrian Count and his faithful companion von Hoenel were marching across this same desert without knowing whether in fact a lake would be found at the end of their trek—they had entered this dread territory "blind." But he at least knew of the existence of Lake Rudolf—thanks largely to their enterprise. So long as he kept going, and on the right compass-bearing, he would, apart from some unforeseen disaster, eventually reach his objective, the so-called Jade Sea.

They came unexpectedly on a native fisherman, of the Turkana tribe, asleep on the bank of a lugga. So sound asleep was he that to wake him one of the camel men put a pinch of fine dust in his nostrils, so that he woke himself with a violent sneeze.

There was a good reason for waking him. For not only had he some fish with him—which indicated that there must be water within, say, a day's march—but he had some goatskins full of water. When he had recovered from his astonishment at being wakened, he told them where he had obtained the water. It was from a spring he knew of, not far from this very spot. Then a look of cunning came into his eyes. He spotted Hillaby's Winchester rifle, and made it clear that what he wanted above all was some fresh meat. If the white man would shoot some for him. . . .

This seemed a fair exchange. Hillaby and one of the camel men set off, and were lucky enough to spot a young duiker, or antelope. Inexperienced as he was, Hillaby brought it to the ground with his first shot. The Turkana was delighted. The happy outcome of this chance encounter was that the camel men were able to load up with as much water as they could carry, obtained from a spring to which the man led them, and which they would have almost certainly missed altogether if they had not met him. And the man himself wandered off with the carcass slung across his bent shoulders, the prospect of a good meal dominating his thoughts.

It seemed to matter less now that the ground continued to slope upwards, away from the lugga. Their thirst was quenched, and they had plenty of water in reserve. True, the Longippi Hills and Kulal, their important landmarks, still lay far ahead of them to the north, but their summits were high, and they stood out boldly, as though encouraging them onward. Beyond them, unless he had hopelessly misjudged his direction, Lake Rudolf would surely be located. But by now, Hillaby had realized how difficult it is to judge distance over desert terrain. The hills were certainly there, but—how far away were they? It was no use asking any of the camel men. Their reply would be, as always, "not very far." That could mean anything!

The first indication they had that they really were nearing

Lake Rudolf was when they saw ahead of them a curious and unexpected pattern of cairns, each of them about twelve feet in diameter. Hillaby was enormously relieved at seeing these, for he had been told before setting out that this group of cairns lay right on the route he should be taking, and within a comparatively short distance of his objective. They were believed to be memorials to the dead erected by members of the Turkana tribe in the distant past, and by a neighboring tribe, the Elmolo, whose territory skirted the southern shores of the lake. Hillaby noticed that only the leading camel man would go anywhere near them, the others were far too superstitious. He himself, to the ill-concealed anxiety of the men, climbed laboriously to the top of one of the cairns in the hope of picking out the route more clearly, or even making out in the far distance water glinting beneath the sun.

The going now was very bad. Indeed, unless it could be explained by their mounting weariness after so many days of hard slogging over rough ground and beneath unbearable heat, it was worse than any they had encountered so far. And it seemed to be becoming worse all the time. Fortunately the sandstorm had blown itself out, but the hot wind still blew on their flanks, continuously urging the camels off the track they should be following. As a result, the camel men expended an immense amount of energy in man-handling them, beating their lank shanks, tugging at their headropes and yelling at them in the lingo which, apparently, was the only one the beasts understood, whether they obeyed the instructions or not.

From time to time they came to a complete halt. During the earlier stages of the trek, when they had halted, the camels immediately foraged for scrub on which to browse. On these later halts, however, two or three or more of them invariably flopped down on their bellies as though determined never to rise to their feet again. The effort of getting them on the move each time exasperated everyone, and for the first time Hillaby found himself becoming irritable and losing the buoyancy that had seen him through all the trials that had beset him up until now.

There was another member of the party now. A Turkana tribesman had, without invitation, decided to join them. He proved to be a most useful guide, for he knew the region better than any of the others. He led them to the Sirima track, and they realized that without his expert assistance they would probably have missed it altogether. After a while he led them somewhat off the track and onto what appeared to be a very uninviting ridge of bare rock that protruded like a blunt knife-edge from the surrounding lava. It was harder walking than ever, but at least it was free of boulders, though these lay on either side of it like the petrified corpses of fabulous monsters long since dead.

After several hours he came to an abrupt halt. He pointed forward. The party followed with bloodshot eyes the line in which he was pointing. There was a gorge straight ahead of them, perhaps five or six miles distant. Shading his eyes, Hillaby strove to pierce the haze. He thought—though he could not be sure—that he could catch a glimpse of water on the far side of the gorge.

Their Turkana guide, whom they had named Ikky, then made it clear that his services were at an end—he wanted now to return to his own people. An unmistakable question hung in the air: the anticipated reward for those services. Hillaby gave the man some sticks of dried camel meat, some fish-hooks and a length of fishing-line. To Ikky, this was manna from heaven. He snatched at the gifts, at infinite risk of embedding the barbed fish-hooks in the palm of his hand. Then, without a word, he turned on his heel and strode purposefully back along the ridge of rock they had all been following.

They marched on toward the entrance to the gorge, following the last miles of the Sirima track. Soon the towering walls of basalt began to close in on either side of them.

They felt that they were walking deliberately into a vast oven. But there was no alternative if they were to reach the water. Now they could clearly see it, glinting ahead of them. For the first time on this journey the camel men's invariable comment, "not very far," could be seen to be true.

It was nearly the hour of sunset when they had finished marching through the gorge. They knew that if they kept going, they must inevitably reach the edge of the lake. They had complete confidence in Ikky, their Turkana guide. He had promised them that the lake would be there. When they reached it, they would not only have as much water to drink as they wanted, but they could wash, could take refuge from the heat and the sand in the sweltering air by immersing themselves completely!

And so, at long last, they came to Lake Rudolf, the Jade Sea. In the warm light of the setting sun behind their shoulders it fully lived up to its romantic name, for it lay like a vast jewel in a multi-colored setting which seemed composed of every hue in the rainbow. Scenting water, the camels increased their stride. Their drivers, knowing that there was now no risk of their straying from the route to one side or the other, released their headropes and abandoned them to their own whims. Then, their loose sandals flapping on their heels, they set off at full speed for the edge of the lake.

Hillaby felt in himself a mounting excitement, that of a dream at last come true. His weariness forgotten, he raced after them. Close behind them, he came to the water's edge and plunged in, clothes and all, to exchange the heat and dryness of the desert air for the welcome cool embrace of the lake itself. As he plunged in, and began to swim into deeper, cooler water, he realized that he was wearing a wristwatch, and that it was not a waterproof one. But this was no moment to worry about such a minor detail: he had reached Lake Rudolf, and that was all that mattered! The fact that he had ahead of him a return trek of another five or six hundred miles was something else that he would thrust from his mind. For the time being he would revel in the caress of the waters of the Jade Sea at sundown, and in his justifiable sense of triumph. The future could look after itself!

John Hillaby continued his exploration of the region whose focal point for him was 'The Jade Sea' by striking onwards and upwards into what are known as the Hurri Hills. Not until early February, when he had completed his wanderings in the region and thoroughly explored the western coastline of the lake itself, did he turn back and head once more for his starting-point, Wamba. He arrived there just before the last day of the month, fit and well in spite of the arduous trek; but three of his camels failed to survive—which says something for the toughness as well as the determination of this explorer!

André Migot in Bandit Country

In 1946 a Frenchman, Dr. André Migot, set out on a remarkable journey, largely on foot, along the tracks to be found threading the mountain passes and valleys that constitute much of the borderland between Western China and Eastern Tibet. It was a journey involving so much hardship, such near-superhuman physical effort and stamina, so many hazards and very real dangers, that it occupied much of that year and the following one.

Migot was an archaeologist and anthropologist. He spoke a number of languages, and what is just as important, had a remarkable gift for coming to terms with tribesmen who until his unexpected arrival in their territory, had rarely if ever had any contact at all with Westerners. He possessed immense courage, fortitude and resourcefulness. It was not in his makeup ever to admit defeat—though, as this part of his long journey reveals, he came perilously near to doing so. As a result, he triumphed over all the obstacles that lay, or were placed, in his path, and completed his extraordinary journey and the research that was its mainspring. One of the most dramatic stages of the journey, which began at Kunming, in Yunnan Province, and ended at Koko Nor in Chinghai Province, was that which lay between Ya-an and K'angting.

The so-called road, part of which Migot had traveled over while perched precariously on an ancient truck carrying freight and a human cargo northward from Sichang, ended abruptly at Ya-an. And it was here that the fairly level agricultural land they had so far passed through began to

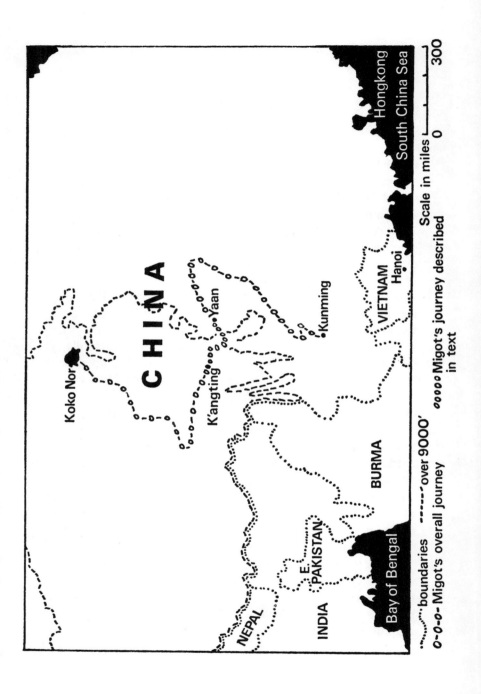

change. To begin with there were low foothills, then there were real hills, and in the distance there were the first true mountains, and no further road was practicable. From this point on the man who wished to penetrate farther to the north and west could do so only on foot and with ever-increasing difficulty. Migot well knew this. But all his life it had been his way to accept challenges, and even to seek them out for the sheer joy of triumphing over them.

In Ya-an he made inquiries among the natives about the terrain through which he would be traveling for, he estimated, the next two or three months at least, if not a great deal longer. He learned that the wealthy Chinese merchants who occasionally made this journey always traveled by "hua kan," an elaborate carrying-chair mounted on the back of a coolie, with a second coolie alongside to steady it on the worst stretches of track and to relieve his companion at intervals when the load he was carrying had reduced him to a state of complete exhaustion.

Migot could not bear the thought of allowing a fellow human-being, even though he would be well accustomed to such labor, to carry his weight up and down the mountain trails that lay ahead of him. He was used to traveling rough, to relying on the muscles of his legs to transport him over all sorts and conditions of terrain. He would make use of them here, then, as he had done so often in the past in other countries.

Ya-an was a market town where traders from China met and haggled and bartered with traders from Tibet. Talking and listening carefully to men such as these, Migot picked up a good deal of information about the route he would be following. As he did so, he was laying in provisions and equipment for his journey. He was also on the lookout for a coolie or two who would accompany him for the initial stages at any rate, and serve both as guides and as carriers. His route was familiar to many of them, for it lay along one of the traditional "tea-routes," on which long lines of coolies struggled day after day, week after week, between Chengtu and K'angting.

Struggled is certainly the word to use. For the China tea they transported on their backs into Tibet was made up into solid "bricks," which in turn were packed into rectangular blocks weighing up to about twenty-six pounds each. A coolie would be loaded with as many of these twenty-six-pound packs as he could be persuaded to carry on his pack-frame, and would then be dispatched northward to his destination in company with ten or a dozen others. Every laborer, that is every coolie, in the area, therefore, was well used to continuous hard going beneath back-breaking loads. It was not difficult to find two who would be willing to accompany him, very much heavily loaded, and for the promise of generous reward.

On March 24th, Migot and his two coolies set off westward from Ya-an, heading for the Tibetan border. Almost from the start, however, he was not entirely happy in his mind about the coolies. They did not look strong—though he knew by now that a Westerner is not capable of assessing the physical qualities of a Chinese, for their skinny, almost fleshless legs often prove to be as strong and resistant to hardship as the finest tensile steel. It was not only that. He was a little unhappy about their attitude toward him as soon as they were well away from their base. They were grasping in the matter of payment, obviously aware that they were employed now by someone more likely to be easily imposed upon than were the hard-bitten Chinese tea merchants and other employers of coolie labor. Migot told himself that these were the men he had employed, and he must therefore make the best of them and not allow himself to be mastered by them.

The first day's traveling, as far as the village of Tienshuan, was comparatively easy. The foothills were gentle, almost inviting. There were well-tilled fields lying in the smooth valley bottoms, and the landscape was dotted with the humble dwellings of the peasants who worked in the fields. But within a very short time of setting out, at seven o'clock, on the second morning, it was obvious that the country was about to change, and change dramatically, in character. Gone were the tilled fields, the snug farmsteads, the small, tidy villages, the gently flowing streams. The track was degenerating fast into a tumble of loose boulders, many of them quite evidently brought down the mountainsides by avalanches—some of them obviously of fairly recent occurrence.

Soon the track ran along the side of a river gorge, sometimes appearing to have been hacked bodily out of the rock wall. Here and there it was actually supported by ramshackle scaffolding made of bent poles lashed together with crudely fashioned rope. There were no more villages, now. Occasionally there would be an isolated hovel, built into the side of the hill and giving every indication of being occupied by the poorest of the poor. There was practically no sign of life anywhere. When a man or woman did appear for a moment, to stare across at the little convoy of one Westerner and two attendant coolies straggling behind him, there was no look of welcome, or even of interest, in their dead eyes. Although Ya-an lay only a day and a half's march behind them, there was already an air of desolation, even of menace, pervading the whole landscape.

The two coolies had long before made it clear that they were lazy. They did not act as guides, in spite of their promises before they set out. With every laborious mile covered, they dropped farther and farther behind. Migot knew, however, that for the time being there was no risk that they would actually desert him and make off into the mountains with his stores and equipment, for he had taken the precaution of paying them only a small part of the wage on which they had agreed. The rest was to be paid when this particular stage of his journey was completed and he enlisted the services of a fresh escort. He suspected that their awkwardness, after starting, about the matter of payment was connected with a possible intention on their part of abandoning him and stealing his goods.

They came at the end of that day to what passed for a village in those remote and inhospitable parts. It was a cluster of poor hovels, one of which, he was given to understand, could offer some sort of accommodation. It was only four o'clock in the afternoon, and he had really intended to continue until nightfall, having been told of a larger village, with an inn where he would be able to sleep and eat fairly well. Having eaten nothing at all since setting out from Tienshuan early that morning, he was already hungry. This was hardly surprising, for he had been continuously on the march, on a stony, undulating mountain-foothill track for something like nine hours, and on an empty stomach. He was tempted to call a halt, but some instinct in him told him that it would be better to continue on his way to the next village.

While he was debating this with himself, his coolie escort caught up with him. They too were tired and hungry, they said. In fact, they said, they were too exhausted to go a yard further along the trail. They thought it wise to stay right here, in this village, where they could eat and sleep. And to make their feelings absolutely clear, they threw down their loads, obtained some rice and without more ado set to work to prepare themselves a meal. Migot thought that perhaps when they had eaten they might be willing to press on for a couple of hours or so to the next village, the one he had told them they must reach that evening. But it was evident that the coolies had made up their minds. There they were, and there they would stay for the night.

Migot accepted the inevitable, though with reluctance. He ate a meal that consisted of a bowl of rice in which a revolting piece of fat pork was embedded. He washed it down with a drink of the sort of tea that is favored in those parts—a strong brew mixed with rancid yak's-milk butter—

and decided to go to bed and try to sleep in readiness for what he knew would be an even more strenuous day to come. He was given a cell-like, windowless room. It was so dark that he did not realize just how filthy and insect-ridden it was until it was too late. The adjoining and larger room was filled to capacity with a horde of natives and coolies, most of whom were smoking opium pipes. The sweet, pungent stench of these conflicted with the many other smells, of human sweat and cooking-fat, that seemed to have impregnated the very floor, walls and ceiling of his own small room. So, he drifted off at last into an uncomfortable sleep, wrapping the folds of his sleeping-bag closely about him.

He was awakened the next morning at six o'clock by the sounds of pandemonium not far away. There were cries and the sound of blows, a barking of dogs and a scuffling of feet in the mud outside and inside the wretched building in which he had spent the night. Migot leaped out of his sleeping-bag and raced into the outer room where he found his coolies in a state of panic-stricken terror. They told him that the village had been invaded by a gang of bandits and murderers, armed to the teeth and bent on robbery with violence. Already they had invaded the room where provisions and equipment had been stored for the night—under their faithful protection, the coolies emphasized repeatedly —and every article they possessed was even now being snatched away.

Migot acted promptly and fearlessly. Rushing out, he tackled the bandits boldly, single-handed. There was just the chance, he thought, that his coolies were mistaken and that this was in fact an official raid by men on the watch for known opium smugglers on the tea-route. He soon realized that this was not so. One of the men, as savage looking a fellow as one might hope to meet anywhere, swung around and demanded the key of the one piece of baggage he possessed which he always kept locked. It contained his precious Leica camera, film and other accessories essential for his work. If there was one thing he was determined not to surrender, it was this key.

He burst into a spate of words. For a moment the bandit looked in surprise that a Westerner could speak a language he understood. Then, with a violent gesture, he made it clear that it was a matter of surrendering that key—or else. Migot stood his ground. But the man was not beaten. For an answer, he snatched up the piece of baggage, slung it over his shoulder, and vanished through the doorway with a cry of triumph. With remarkable courage, Migot leaped after him, caught up with him in the village street and snatched the bag from his shoulder. The man swung around and raced back after him to the hovel, where the two coolies clustered in the doorway, too terrified to do anything to help. And there Migot had to admit defeat, for now the bandit was joined by some of his fellows, and to have resisted further would have been suicidal.

He was stripped of his clothes and then thrown to the ground. The key was located in an inner pocket. With a shout of triumph, the bandit opened the bag and turned it upside down. From where he lay on the beaten mud floor of the hut, Migot had the misery of watching his precious camera being dropped, picked up, shaken, forcibly opened and then tossed to one of the other men. He saw his spools of film, some of them exposed but the greater number of them as yet unused as he was saving them for use in connection with the work he had to do in Tibet, opened and scattered about the room. Even if, after they had gone, he could collect some of these spools of film, they were probably all ruined, now. And in any case it was unlikely that his camera would be spared. One of the bandits, he noticed, had obviously recognized it as an article of value, if only for bartering purposes. He was unlikely to hand it back to him. And since all his money had been taken, he could not even offer to buy it back from the man who had so ruthlessly stolen it.

Now his baggage generally was being torn apart. His shoes had already been removed from his feet, but now his spare pairs also went. He had the ironic task of explaining to their new owners the difference between left foot and right foot, and of matching the shoes for their benefit. As soon as the bandits had satisfied themselves that they had gotten hold of all his belongings they turned their attention to the building in which they had found them. Rice, cooking-utensils, blankets, articles of clothing belonging to the owner and other occupants of the place were snatched up. At the back of the building was a shed with two pigs in it—their most valued possessions. The two pigs, and all the fowls from a poultry-run close to the sty, were seized and carried off.

Not content with that, the bandits next turned their attention on the remaining hovels that composed the ramshackle village, and systematically denuded them of their contents. Their owners were clearly too terrified of the men to put up even a token show of resistance. Nor was this surprising, for by now the bandits numbered about fifty, the vanguard having been joined soon afterward by others of this notorious mountain gang. They were all well armed. They carried an impressive armory of sharp knives and curved daggers in the sashes they wore. In addition to these glistening weapons, their traditional knives, several of the men were armed either with rifles of Chinese manufacture or with heavy German Mauser rifles.

One man, obviously from the respect the others showed him, their leader, carried an even more sinister weapon: an automatic carbine of American manufacture. Even to have pretended to put up a show of resistance in these circumstances, Migot realized, would have been fatal. It would have invited them to indulge in outright murder. He wondered how he had gotten away with his first impulsive act, when he had run boldly out into the street and snatched his precious bag off the shoulder of one of these well armed and obviously ruthless men.

Stripped of everything but his shirt, trousers and socks, Migot watched the bandits at their work. He was just thinking, or at least hoping, that they had done with him, when two of them suddenly came in again. He suspected that they were after his trousers. His Leica camera was slung over one man's shoulder, and he was also wearing his spectacles. The other man was holding up his wallet, with a grin of satisfaction on his weatherbeaten face. He was also brandishing a stick, which Migot recognized as his tent pole. Once more they "frisked" him, as though they believed there might still be something worth stealing tucked into the folds of his shirt. This was hardly likely, for by then it seemed every single one of the bandits had already thrust his grimy fingers at least once into every pocket and cranny of his garments. There was nothing at all left in them now.

Then, quite unexpectedly, there was a complete change of mood. A group of the bandits returned to the building and proceeded to cook some of the eggs they had just stolen. Migot, who had eaten nothing since the bowl of rice and fat pork the night before, watched them preparing the meal with greedy eyes. For many hours past, his stomach had been protesting. One of the bandits looked up, and beckoned to him to join them. It was an odd form of hospitality, considering that they were a band of ruthless thieves and potential murderers. But he was far too hungry to allow such considerations to make him decline their invitation. Most willingly he joined them at the meal.

The final blow was one that in spite of what it meant to him raised a smile. His two coolies, who had not joined them at the table, were ordered to load themselves with the booty won in this dawn raid on the village, including both his own property and what had been ransacked elsewhere. Then, with ropes around their necks so that they could not escape among the mountains, they were led away by the bandits to their own hideout from which they had descended to raid the village in the first light of morning.

Migot was torn in his feelings. The men had not served him well, and he could not really feel sorry for them at the turn of events. Indeed, if they had not laid down their loads and insisted on spending the night in that village this would never have happened. On the other hand, he was now without the small assistance that they had been providing him. As guides they had been useless and as escorts very little use either. But now he was on his own, entirely. He speculated as to whether they might make a desperate attempt at escape, knowing that in all probability they would meet an unpleasant fate when they arrived at the bandits' mountain hideout. Watching, he did see one of them begin to lag behind, as they had so consistently done during the two days' marching that lay behind them. But he saw also the quick glint of a sharp knife as its point was applied to the coolie's back, and the man increased his speed to a brisk trot, till his neckrope brought him up short once more.

Now the last of the bandits had vanished up the winding mountain trail. Dr. Migot was left in the village, to consider what to do next. He had on a pair of worn socks, a very old and tattered pair of trousers, a thin, torn shirt—that was all. Relief at being still alive, even though bereft of almost everything with which he had set out on this long, lonely trek, was an emotion that was fairly soon balanced by a severe fit of shivering. It was still only late March and he was now high up among the mountains. The thin early morning air, now that all the excitement of the raid had ended, was bitterly cold.

He sat down and took stock of what he had lost. All the money he had brought with him for a journey of unknown duration was gone: the gold bars—which in some parts were the only currency acceptable to the natives he would meet, the United States dollars, the Chinese dollars, the English pound sterling. All his clothes, save for the few he stood up in, had gone. He had no shoes. The sweaters he had brought for use when the weather became really cold in the high mountains had been taken. His camping-kit, including his invaluable sleeping-bag, had gone with the rest. He had lost his precious medicine-chest, his maps, a revolver, a carbine, and ammunition for both weapons. For the bandits, he reflected, this must have been one of the most rewarding dawn raids they had ever carried out. Perhaps that was why they had so unexpectedly invited him to share their breakfast? He was truly grateful to them for that gesture.

It occurred to him that there was always the slender chance that they might have dropped something while making their getaway from the vilage. Or they might even have deliberately jettisoned some articles for which they could think of no use. It was just as well that Migot had this idea, for it turned out to be a rewarding one.

Having given them plenty of time to get away, he set off up the track they had taken, feeling his way cautiously in his stockinged feet. He had not gone very far before he came across, of all invaluable articles, his small tent. Though there was no sign of the tent pole, this was immensely encouraging. He could surely fashion for himself a new pole, and with a tent he could at least count on some sort of protection from the elements and shelter for the night between villages. He found, too, a couple of tins of jam and a container of salt, and smiled wryly at the kind of meal he would be able to prepare from that assortment of ingredients. More important, though, he found his passport, lying half-hidden among the stones of the mountain track. Opening it, he found that his photograph had been torn from it before the passport itself was thrown away. Grinning to himself, he said that it was obvious that one of the bandits had taken a fancy to him and was retaining the photo as a reminder of the "friend" he had so completely denuded of his possessions!

With the tent on his shoulder, and a stick in his hand, Migot lost no more time, but set out along the track in the direction of the village he had intended to reach the night before. Again he reminded himself that but for the obstinacy of those two coolies of his all this might have been avoided. And then he reflected—it was quite possible that word had reached the bandits in their mountain lair, traveling as news seems to do in the unlikeliest places and by the most mysterious means, that a Westerner, well equipped and with an unusually small escort, was now on his way from Tien-shuan, bound for K'angting. It was quite possible that some of the bandits had been shadowing him from higher up the mountainside, waiting from one hour to the next until they could agree on the best point from which to make their swoop. They had been fortunate in that he had broken off his day's march early, but if he had continued to the next village they could always have continued to watch from a distance, and swoop there instead.

So far as the ground was concerned, with its rough stones, its loose boulders and its intermittent tumbling streams to ford, the going was as hard as ever. It was made harder, of course, by the fact that Migot was having to walk in his stocking-feet. But he was to have a stroke of luck. After some hours of painful walking he came to a small encampment of Chinese soldiery. They had been alerted by the sound of gunfire in the region and had been told to make a foray into this part of the mountains. The gunfire, Migot supposed, had been a letting-off of rifles and other weapons to signal the triumphant foray the bandits had made into that village.

The officer in command was sympathetic. He ordered that a lavish bowl of rice and meat should be cooked for their unexpected guest. He also provided a pair of the surprisingly tough straw sandals worn by natives in the mountains. Fortified by the meal, and with something to protect his feet at last, Migot set off westward again. He had been told that the soldiers' headquarters would be found not many miles along the track, at a place named Chussekuan. There, he was assured, everything possible would be done for his comfort and well-being.

He arrived in due course at Chussekuan, and there the officer's promises were amply fulfilled. He was given the best meal he had had for a long time past. An army greatcoat was thrown about his shoulders to cover the tattered shirt that was all he had to protect him from the cold. Better still, the headquarters were in communication by telegraph-line with Chengtu, the nearest town of any size, and a message was sent to the French Consul in residence there, acquainting him with what had happened to this French traveler. A room was placed at his disposal and he was told that he could remain at the headquarters as long as he liked—or at least until facilities had been obtained for him to continue on his way.

One thing that perhaps surprisingly worried Migot at this time was the matter of his two coolies. It was true that they had not been of much use to him. But strictly speaking, since they were in his employ he was responsible for their safety. He discussed this aspect of the situation with the commanding officer, but was advised by him not to do anything in too much of a hurry. Migot understood. He was a seasoned traveler who knew well that it was folly ever to show a desire for speed and expedition in such country. Better by far to adapt oneself to the prevailing tempo and to await events with as much fatalism, or at least resignation, as one could muster. The thought that he was at one end of a telegraph line was a great comfort to him.

So, he lingered on. In view of the loss of his money he would, he realized, have to curtail the scope of his journey as originally planned. Perhaps now he would have to give up his aim of reaching far-distant Sinkiang, and eventually India itself? But he could surely arrange, by a telegraphed message, to have some money sent to him at, say, K'angting, the end of the present stage of his journey? And some more money at, say, Sining. This would enable him to reach Jyekundo and Koko Nor, two of the points in this remote and desolate region which he was determined by hook or by crook to reach. The thought that he would perhaps not have to admit defeat and turn about after all was one that warmed him during the long cold night that followed his arrival at the soldiers' headquarters at Chussekuan.

The next day was a very long one indeed. There was nothing that he could do, and he found the continuous toing-and-fro-ing among various possibilities even more frustrating, even more exhausting, than he had found the barefoot slogging of the previous day's march. Toward the end of that day, however, he had a surprise. His two coolies suddenly turned up, "out of the blue." Dusk had fallen when filthy as ever they appeared at the soldiers' quarters. They were utterly exhausted, and in a state of dilapidation even worse than when he had last seen them, roped together, on the mountain trail to the bandits' lair. He was not sure whether he was relieved or otherwise to see them again. On the whole, perhaps in view of his sense of responsibility, he was relieved.

They threw themselves down on the ground close to a fire, and moaned piteously about their plight. They had, they said, been forced to carry their captors' booty up a steep mountain trail for at least five hours. It was well after midday when they reached their hiding-place. Every time they had slowed down—and Migot could guess, from his own experiences with them, just how often that would have been—they were savagely beaten with sticks. They had been continuously threatened with death at the end of the trail if they did not keep going. Their backs had been almost broken by the weight they were forced to carry. They had been given nothing to eat or drink. Having reached their captors' mountain hideout they had been immediately turned adrift, still without food, and told to make themselves scarce without delay. If they were still within earshot inside a quarter of an hour they could expect to be pursued and shot outright. The bandits' leader had tapped his automatic carbine meaningfully as he spoke, and the two coolies knew better than to doubt that he would carry out his threat without the slightest hesitation.

When at last it was possible to continue on his journey, Migot paid off one of the two men, the older and more troublesome, having decided that he could press on with better prospects of success if he retained only the younger man. He had now arranged for money to be deposited in his name at K'angting and at another place. Having replaced the most essential items of his lost equipment with what he could raise at the soldiers' headquarters, he felt confident that he could make fair progress with one companion. It would be easier to keep him up to scratch since he would not have an ally in the other and older coolie, now paid off.

For some time they now shared the trail with a convoy of rich merchants, each of whom was traveling in the traditional fashion, carried on the back of a sweating coolie. He noticed that these men all looked scornfully down on him as he stumbled along the trail, obviously regarding him as no better than the coolies staggering beneath their weight, or even the beasts in the convoy carrying the heavier loads. There was never a smile or a kindly look from any of them. Their coolie-carriers staggered along at a brisk pace, and Migot realized that ill-equipped as he now was, and having already been attacked once by mountain bandits, he would be wise to remain as close as possible to this numerous and well-furnished convoy.

It distressed him deeply, though, to see how the chair coolies were treated. All the occupants of these hua kans were massive, heavily built and sumptuously clothed figures. Most of them, he estimated, must weigh anything up to three hundred pounds. Yet in all the time that he was with this convoy he never once saw one of the merchants permit his carrier to set down his burden and take a rest. Never once did one of them, even on the steepest parts of the trail, where the stony track seemed to corkscrew its way up to the very sky, condescend to step out of his chair and relieve his coolie of his enormous weight. He could tell from the coolies' drawn faces that their lungs were ready to burst with the strain of hoisting such immense human loads up such steep gradients in the biting, rarefied mountain air. The muscles in their thin calves stood out like knotted cords, and there were horrifying varicose veins in almost every one of them. He remembered that he had been recommended to hire a hua kan for his own use on this trail, and was glad that he had declined the suggestion.

From time to time they encountered other convoys of coolies manhandling gigantic loads of China brick-tea. One such convoy was encountered on a mountain pass where the trail was nine thousand feet above sea level, high above a deep, canyon-like valley where a false step would mean certain death on the crags many thousands of feet below. It was so cold here that there was ice on the track. There were enormous icicles, like ancient stalactites, hanging from the rock edges at the side of the trail. The coolies' straw sandals, and in many cases bare feet, had trodden out a hollow path in the winding track. In this, Migot, not yet accustomed to the clumsy straw sandals he had been given, slipped and slithered and stumbled. By now they had rubbed his feet into blisters. The blisters continually burst, so that blood flowed and congealed beneath and on top of his feet. They were so cold, however, that he could hardly feel any pain, but he was conscious of a deadness that was more alarming than painful, because he knew it could mean the onset of frostbite. This, unless it was mastered in its earliest stages, would lead almost certainly to eventual amputation —if he was to avoid gangrene spreading through his whole system, the end result of which could only be death.

At times the mountain trail was so steep that these load-carrying coolies, tough as they were, had to dump their tea-brick loads, halve them, and make a double journey up each stretch of the track, carrying first one half and then the other, to unite them with rope at the top, reload, and carry on until the gradient became too steep once more. Migot estimated that even these half-loads must weigh at least a hundred pounds apiece. That was a weight heavy enough to break a man's back even on level ground and a surface easy to walk on. It was a long time since he had seen such a surface as that, and it would be a long time before these coolies came to such a surface.

Each man carried an iron-shod staff. When sheer exhaustion obliged him to halt, and he did not feel he had the strength to pick up his load if he once let it fall to the ground, he would place his staff behind him and then lean back in such a way that part of the weight of his load was supported by it. In that way he could rest until such time as he felt able to continue on his journey. There was the constant fear, of course, of being separated from his companions and so risking an attack from the mountain bandits, so a coolie had to be in dire straits indeed to linger for more than a few seconds at a time to recoup his strength.

The journeys they were ordered to take by their employers could last weeks, even months, and had to be carried out in every kind of weather. Watching them, Migot had to admit that by contrast his own self-imposed trek was less terrible as an ordeal. The coolies were, he realized, nothing more than beasts-of-burden. It was small wonder that when their interminable day's march was over they sought release from their exhaustion and hunger by smoking pipe after pipe of opium. In that way, and that way only, could they find temporary oblivion.

Still the long trail climbed, approaching the higher reaches of the mountains that barred the way to secret Tibet. He became separated from the convoy of merchants, officials and businessmen with whom for a while he had shared the trail. He was long accustomed to the contemptuous glances they cast upon him as he plodded along, often forced to one side or the other by the chair carriers, who knew that if they did not demand the easiest and safest portions of the track they might jolt their employers, and be brutally punished as a result. He had become an object of derision. The old army greatcoat which he had been given at the soldiers' headquarters, and for which he had been so grateful as the cold grew more and more intense, seemed to be the focal point in their idle mockery of this Westerner plodding along in his clumsy straw sandals on the trail they felt they owned. Mockery is often harder to endure than hostility, and it did not help Migot during this interminable stage in his lonely mountain trek to be repeatedly scorned by these comfortable, affluent men in their hua kans.

By the end of yet another day's march his straw sandals had practically disintegrated. Both feet were now masses of running sores. The many blisters had met and merged with one another and blood and mucus flowed from them. His coolie companion had flagged more and more throughout the day. Now he declared that he could not and would not carry even the small amount of food and equipment that had been allocated to him. Migot said nothing, but simply added that burden to his own. Perhaps he hoped to shame the man by doing so, but if so he was mistaken. Small as it was, compared with what had been his property when they set out from Ya-an all those eventful days ago, it was almost more than he could manage, for he was no longer as fit and strong as when he had set out on his trek.

They encountered two herdsmen. Speaking a dialect he could not easily follow, they told the coolie that if they branched off the trail a hundred yards farther on they would come to a shortcut that would save them a great deal of hard going. Assuming that the information was correct, Migot agreed to the coolie's insistence that they should try this new route. They came to the fork in the trail and followed the alternative. It led them to a completely impassable barrier, and they had no choice but to return to their original trail. The fact that this involved a steep climb back made this episode all the more bitter. They had lost a great deal of time and expended a great deal of effort—and had nothing to show for it at all.

It was after darkness had fallen that day that they eventually stumbled upon a tiny community of Chinese men, women and children, in a hovel not far from the track. By then it was impossible to go any farther, for the track was difficult and dangerous enough even when the light was good. They entered the hovel. Some of the Chinese scattered about on the mud floor wriggled to one side to make room for the newcomers. And there Migot and his coolie companion slept a fitful sleep of utter exhaustion until the first glint of light the next morning. Then they struggled to their feet, thanked their hosts, and picked their way out from among them and once more took up the mountain trail.

There was another day to face. Migot estimated that K'angting was still a hundred miles and more to the west. That meant several days' march ahead of them. The only comfort he had was the sure knowledge that with every laborious and painful mile covered they were that much nearer to the Tibetan frontier, his objective. But with his feet in this state, he began seriously to wonder whether he would be able to cover a hundred miles and more of mountain track. Every step he now took was an agony. The sores on his feet were open and running. Some of them were festering, and he realized that they could well have become poisoned by the soil that rubbed into them and by the scraping of twigs and thorns when their trail led them through undergrowth. They spent the night too on the mud floor of the Chinese hovel.

One night they stopped in a squalid rest-house which they unexpectedly found among a group of mountainside hovels. It was dark when they settled in, and pitch dark by the time they had dropped off to sleep. Migot was awakened by the sensation of something crawling over his face and his bare hands and feet. It was as though a course blanket was being dragged across him. He reached out for a candle and lit it. What he then saw was certainly no blanket. It was a swarm of insects packed so closely that they seemed to move across him as though knit together. They were in fact bed-bugs, swarming out of the cracks between the planks.

In fact, this was to prove the last really bad night—at least on this memorable stage of his journey. In the morning he found that his feet were now so bad that for the first time he had to decide on some mode of transport. He sent the coolie ahead, with the promise of a bonus payment, to arrange for a hua kan to be sent back down the trail in order that he could be carried over the last remaining miles to K'angting. He hated the very thought of this, especially after what he had seen when he was with the convoy of merchants, but he now had to accept the inevitable. At K'angting he knew that he would be able to rest, to eat well, and above all receive medical treatment so that his feet would heal and he could build up his strength for the next stage of his journey.

Meanwhile, to save time and occupy his mind, he doctored his feet as best he could. He repaired his badly worn straw sandals, and then set out, very slowly, picking his way carefully along the trail, to meet the hua kan he had ordered. He had the ability, in spite of the extreme pain his feet were giving him, to take in the extraordinary beauty of the valley that lay spread out below the track he was follow-ing. It was enclosed by steep mountainsides, and at the upper end of it, gleaming like silver in the sunlight, was the nose of a great glacier. Beyond that were the upper slopes of a mountain peak whose topmost crags were enveloped in high clouds. Below him he could see a mighty torrent, formed from the melting snows, tearing its way down the valley sides and exploding against the boulders that lay scattered in its path, large as houses and looking as though they had been hurled there in the very dawn of time.

It was soon after he had paused there, resting his aching feet and absorbing the splendor of the mountainscape, that he saw coming toward him a group of men surrounding a hua kan. He realized that it could not possibly be the one that he had sent his coolie to K'angting to summon, so it must be—quite simply—a miracle!

Two missionaries accompanied the coolie carriers. They were not traveling in the hua kan, as the indolent and offensive Chinese merchants and officials had been, but walking sturdily alongside, among the men. The missionaries greeted Dr. Migot in God's name. As they did so, they glanced down and noticed his bleeding feet, from which by now the last vestige of the straw sandals had parted. The older of the two men immediatetly took charge. The man they had so unexpectedly encountered on the trail, and who was so obviously at the end of his strength, must get into the hua kan at once. He would be conveyed back along the trail to their base, a Catholic Mission established among the mountains, and there he would be treated by one of their fellow brethren, a man who was well accustomed to such calls upon his knowledge and expertise. The missionary spoke with authority. Migot did not argue with him.

So, this stage of the long trek through the China-Tibetan borderland ended happily. Dr. Migot was treated, as he knew he would be, with kindness and generosity at the Catholic Mission. The story of his encounter with the bandits, far back along the winding trail, and of the appalling difficulties he had had to face as a direct result of this encounter, was made known to the Chinese authorities.

IN BANDIT COUNTRY

They were deeply concerned that such a misfortune should have come to so distinguished a visitor to their country. Compensation was offered, both in the form of money and in other forms.

It was not a great deal. But it was sufficient to enable Dr. André Migot, when he had recovered from his injuries, to continue on his way with renewed hope and the expectation of ultimate success. His expectation was realized. By the end of the year 1947 he had reached his remote objective, the strange lake at Koko Nor, in the Province of Chinghai. He had completed one of the most remarkable journeys on foot ever undertaken by a Westerner, and in a region where comparatively few Westerners ever set foot at all.

But André Migot's trek was not yet at an end. True, he had reached his first objective, Koko Nor; but by then he was, as it were, "in the middle of nowhere," his task not yet complete. He had been charged by the *Ecole Française d'Extreme-Orient* with the task of carrying out detailed research into the archaeological aspects of the vast territories through which, for most of the time virtually alone, he would be obliged to travel.

This in itself would have been sufficient responsibility for most men, but Migot was intensely interested also in the way of life, and especially the religious way of life, of the Buddhists among whom his way led him. To attain the results which alone would satisfy him he adopted various strategies, including that of disguising himself as a Tibetan mendicant, or wandering friar. Thus disguised, he almost succeeded in entering that Holy of Holies, the city of Lhasa itself. But on the verge of success, his disguise was penetrated, he was unmasked, and had it not been for his obvious piety and love and understanding of the Buddhists and their way of life, would undoubtedly have been put to death.

He was, however, spared, and continued his marathon

journey, eastward now, through Inner Mongolia to the city of Peking. It was now 1948—the year after his long trek to Koko Nor. He was justified in supposing that, once in the Chinese capital, he was safe and would be permitted to travel back to his base in Indo-China. But this was not to be. He was arrested by the Communists and taken by them into the wild mountains of Manchuria, where he underwent further hardships before eventually being released and permitted by his captors to return to base.

Surprisingly—or perhaps not so surprisingly in view of the sort of man he was—instead of now taking the easy and direct way home he chose to travel back across the vast expanse of China the whole way to Eastern Tibet all over again. From there, after a series of hair-raising experiences that compare in drama with those already described, he finally reached his starting-point. In André Migot, Doctor of Medicine and much else, you have an example of a man born to travel—a man for whom no hardship is impossible to bear, no danger too great to face, no challenge too fierce to be accepted and overcome. He was a man whose whole life was eagerly devoted to studying the little-known in the confident hope of widening the horizons of his fellow-men's knowledge of the world and its peoples.

Laurens van der Post in Nyasaland

Laurens van der Post, soldier, prisoner-of-war of the Japanese, traveler, explorer, writer and much else besides, knows the Far East well. He has explored in Ethiopia, in the notorious wastes of the Kalahari Desert and elsewhere in Africa. In the year 1949 the British Government commissioned him to make a survey of a relatively little-known mountainous region in Nyasaland that lies to the south of Lake Nyasa and is almost surrounded by Portuguese East African territory. It had already been surveyed from the air, but had not, up to that time, been sufficiently well charted from the ground.

The region consists largely of a complex of high hills, rising at times to the stature of true mountains, to some nine or even ten thousand feet. The hills are interspersed with deep gorges, with furiously tumbling streams, and sometimes unite to form extensive undulating plateaus at a considerable height. Much of this territory has been developed as forest-bearing land. Some forestry experts consider that it is the finest area of man-controlled forest in the whole continent of Africa. Notable among the trees is a species of cedar, believed to be the only species resistant to the terrible and merciless ravages of the African ant. So important are these cedars that they have taken their name from the mountain complex on which they flourish—they are known as Mlanje Cedars.

Apart from the foresters, few Europeans are familiar with this lonely region. One of the greatest hazards, especially among the peaks and defiles and the high, exposed plateaus, is the unpredictable and violent wind that blows off the

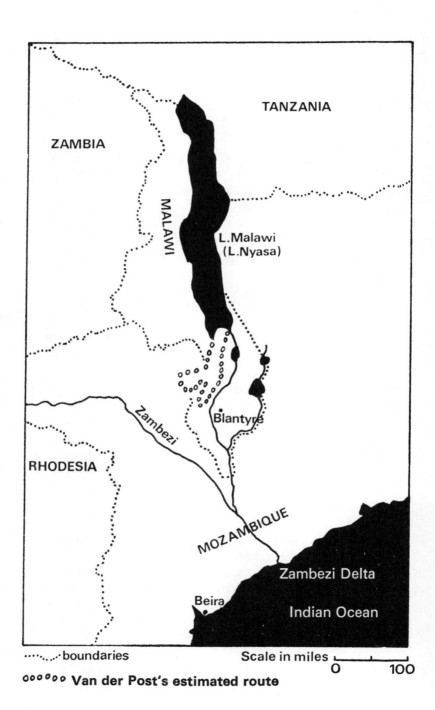

boundaries
∘∘∘∘∘ Van der Post's estimated route
Scale in miles
0   100

mountain peaks of Portuguese East Africa, notably off Mount Chiperone. So terrible are these winds, with the rain they bring, that they are known locally as Chiperones. It is characteristic that they start without warning, blow furiously for five days, and end as suddenly as they began. During those five days anyone caught on the Mlanje will hole-up, for to attempt to move about in such conditions is to invite disaster, and almost certain death. It might be from sheer exposure to the icy and persistent cold. It might be because the force of the wind is sufficient to pick a man up and hurl him bodily two thousand feet off the plateau or slope to the bottom of some craggy gorge. Van der Post was to learn the truth of this, the hard way.

Though he had not previously explored this part of Africa, van der Post was an old campaigner. He knew that ample allowance in regard to time, provisions and equipment must always be made, for hazards and dangers could extend the estimated duration of any trek. So, with the assistance of the District Commissioner and other officers serving in the Protectorate in 1949, he raised a party of some thirty native bearers, good men all of them, and men familiar with the region and the conditions they would have to face. He laid in stores sufficient for a three-week trek, and had these divided into relatively easy loads averaging between forty and fifty pounds for each bearer. That should enable them to maintain a good rate of progress however difficult the going might prove to be.

Among the stores were large quantities of bacon, endless strings of sausages, scores of tins of bully beef, the traveler's traditional standby, enormous quantities of potatoes, bread, flour, beans, peas, biscuits, powdered milk, sardines, jam, butter, coffee, cocoa and tea. There were frying pans, kettles and saucepans, water-containers, stoves, hurricane-lamps, flashlights, coils of manilla rope, knives, a double-barreled shotgun and ammunition, tents, sleeping-bags and groundsheets and a first-aid outfit liberally furnished with drugs.

They set off from the forester's hut at Chambe, the assembly-point for the bearers. Though it was early morning, the sun was bright and strong and the weather fine. In such conditions it was hard to believe—though van der Post knew it must be true—that the mountains on which they were now setting foot could become shrouded in a matter of minutes in wind-driven rain so furious, so all-enveloping, that it was suicide to try to march through it. He remembered how he had been told, by one of the District Commissioner's staff, that the Chiperones develop so suddenly, so swiftly, that they seem to explode into being. It could be brilliantly fine at eleven o'clock in the morning and raining pitilessly within half an hour But on that morning of Monday, May 23rd, some thousands of feet up on the middle slopes of the Mlanje massif, such conditions were unthinkable. They seemed to belong to a completely different world.

The native guide went ahead, with the long train of native carriers strung out behind him, stepping purposefully and cheerfully out along the steeply ascending mountain track. Van der Post, with two other white men, Peter Quillan, the Chief Forestry Officer for the province, and Richard Vance, the local Forestry Officer, delayed their departure from base for a short while. As they were traveling light, they knew they would have time enough to overtake the main body when they halted to pitch their first camp. When they did set out they found that the track, though steep, was not too exacting. They could afford to stop every now and then and look and wonder at the stupendous views that opened out on either side. They estimated that they could see a full hundred miles across the one-thousand-foot plateau to a great range of mountains in Portuguese East Africa, to the Blantyre Hills and the Kirk range itself.

For part of the way, the track they were following was a razor-edge with a drop on each side that Vance estimated at not less than five thousand feet. The only other users of this mountain track proved to be a train of sturdy natives each of whom was carrying, balanced on his head, an enormous load of timber sawed on the site where the Mlanje cedars were being felled higher up the mountain. The poise and sureness of foot that the men exhibited beneath their crushingly cumbersome loads was miraculous. Quillan told van der Post that the men's wages were a few pennies a day, in addition to their food. What astonished him more than anything else, perhaps, was the fact that each native bearer as he went down the track raised one hand in salute and muttered the traditional term of respect for the white man, "Bwana."

They came in time to an area of the Mlanje where the plateau broke up into a scatter of narrow terraces clinging to seven-thousand-foot precipices. Along and up these the sure-footed native carriers climbed, at an almost unvarying pace. From time to time they vanished in dense groves of cedar, to emerge later a thousand feet higher up on the far side. By the end of the day they had covered some thirteen mountain miles, and it was time to pitch camp. Next day they alternately climbed and descended out of and into a succession of steep-sided valleys. In the middle of the day it was blazing hot, even at that height, in the full glare of the sun, and oppressively hot and humid in the shadowed hollows down into which they had so often to climb before ascending to higher reaches beyond.

By late afternoon, however, in the shade especially, the temperature had dropped so far that the carriers, in spite of their strenuous exertions, began to complain bitterly of the increasing cold. Eighteen miles was all they could do that day, a longer one than the first day out had been. Some time before they halted to pitch camp they had passed a ruinous hut in which an old man told them he had lived more than half his life completely alone. He told van der Post that he and his two companions were only the third group of white men who had passed his hut in more than thirty years.

So far the weather had been kind to them, though the alternations of great heat by day and very real cold by night had taxed Quillan and Vance severely. It was nothing new to van der Post, however, for he had had wide experience of the Kalahari and other deserts, and was familiar with this alternating of heat by day and cold by night.

On Friday, May 27th, the three men stood on a ridge that they estimated at about nine thousand feet above sea level. They were confronted with a truly spectacular view. But as they studied it, Quillan pointed out, in a tone that had more of anxiety than appreciation in it, that distant Mount Chiperone was wreathed in mist, its highest peak being in fact completely obliterated. Vance nodded, and pointed out that the wind, such as it was, had been blowing from that very direction. Van der Post caught the word Chiperone being exchanged between his two companions. Quillan, however, suddenly spoke in a reassuring tone—what they could see was no more than a local mist. It would almost certainly dissipate, and they would then see the peaks of Mount Chiperone, as they had done for several days past, completely clear against the sky.

Vance was not happy about this. He had been long enough on the Mlanje massif to know its moods fairly well. On the other hand, he was subordinate to Quillan, and did not like to dispute his word, however doubtful he felt about the judgment. Van der Post, as a newcomer in the district, did not feel that he could challenge it either. But he felt in his bones that the optimism Quillan was now showing did not seem to have much basis. He said nothing. Only time would tell whether Quillan's assessment of the situation was a sound one.

Meanwhile the train of bearers were still forging ahead.

The three men delayed their own departure in order to survey the wonderful gorges and the sinister black-sided precipices of the area. The camp where they planned to spend the night was not more than two hours' march ahead of them, on the far side of a huge plantation of Mlanje cedars. But only a small part of those two hours had elapsed before the three men became conscious of two things: the strength of the light on the mountainside had considerably diminished, and there was an even more startling decrease in the temperature of the air all about them. The two conditions were inseparable, and they had hardly accepted the fact before—like a ghostly gray and sodden blanket—the mist descended upon them and enveloped them.

It thickened immediately, and perceptibly. Within less than a minute they had to draw close together if they were not to lose touch with one another. Then, what had been just damp, clammy air turned to water. The mist became drizzle. By now there was no hint that the sun could still be shining, as it had been only minutes earlier. They lost all sense of direction. Wisely, for the time being at any rate, they deliberately stood stock still. They knew they had come to a halt on the very lip of a gorge three thousand feet deep and almost sheer. At present there was no wind at all, and the situation in which they found themselves was the more uncanny for the absolute silence that now enveloped them with the mist. They felt as though they were cocooned, completely isolated from the rest of the world. Their thirty bearers might have been in another continent altogether.

The whole party had already been on the march, up hill and down, since seven o'clock that morning. It was now just short of noon. The next proposed campsite should not have been far distant—in miles that is, but in these new circumstances it was impossible to tell how long it would take to reach it—if they ever did.

Working by compass, and with infinite caution, the three men now set off in the wake of the bearers, who had not halted on that ridge to look at the view. They tried to "see" through the soles of their boots, to assess in that way the lay of the ground they had to cover. They strained their ears for the sound of a waterfall. This at least would give them some notion as to the sort of terrain close at hand, and whether it was safe or potentially dangerous.

By virtue of the fact that he had organized this expedition, van der Post felt that it was his duty henceforward to make any decisions that had to be made. There was, he said firmly, only one course open to them. Since it was obvious that they were now threatened by the Chiperone wind and rain—for once, it seemed, approaching the Mlanje with some hint of warning—they ought to make for the lower slopes with the least possible delay. He understood that the Chiperone ordinarily concentrated its fury on the peaks and upper slopes and plateau, so the farther they got from these the better. As for the native bearers, they were led by an expert guide. In all probability he had sensed the imminence of the Chiperone before they themselves had, and would have led them to some measure of safety on lower ground. In any case, the three of them could do nothing for the bearers as things stood.

The advice was sound. The three men turned about, and seeking always a stretch of track that descended, slid and scrambled in single file until, quite unexpectedly, they emerged from the enveloping mist as from some evil shroud. Now landmarks became apparent. Though the rain continued to fall, and increased in volume, they could see more or less where they were heading, and did not stumble off the track as they had when they first turned back.

After a while, Vance's sharp ears detected cries in the distance. He recognized the voice of the bearers' guide, who was one of his best men. So the guess that the guide had also turned his party around, to make for the lower slopes of the mountain, had proved sound. The shouts were repeated. The three men followed one another along a non-existent track in the direction of the shouts. In due course they came upon the rest of the party. They had reached a near-level stretch of open ground and were busily erecting makeshift shelters of branches and foliage from the cedars. Into these the whole party crawled, to lie uncomfortably throughout an endless night, listening to the ever-mounting ferocity of the windborne rain lashing the roofs. Van der Post remembered that he had been told that the Chiperone normally blew itself out only at the end of five days. This was only the night of the first day!

As they huddled there, speculating as to their prospects, Richard Vance, the local Forestry Officer, talked about the habits of the animals that frequented the Mlanje when the Chiperone blew. None of them were so hardy as to venture out unless they were near starvation. The leopard, the antelope, the mountain gazelle, the wild pig, even these were all held prisoner until the wind and rain subsided. Foresters had noticed that the leopard, provident against such conditions, used to cache stocks of meat from animals he had killed, so that provided he had gotten back to his lair he had no further need to stir from it to eat till the storm was over.

Tired out from the hard walking and climbing they had done for days past, over terrain that was treacherous and exacting, van der Post and his two companions lay in the rough shelter that their men had erected for them, and listened, and waited. They could not only hear the merciless storm that raged outside, but by laying their ears to the ground they could actually feel the vibrations set up by the furious battering that was being inflicted upon it. There was a steady yet frantic drumming sound, as though from distant native drums sending out their warnings.

By five o'clock next morning none of them could sleep any longer, even though what sleep they had been able to manage was fitful and broken. They discussed what their next move should be. The most direct route back to Chambe, their starting-point, was of course the one by which they had come. But to return by that route would involve climbing those high ridges and "blind" terraces all over again, and in reverse. On the upper levels the Chiperone would be at its most destructive and dangerous. Common sense warned them not to trifle with that notorious and traditional wind.

Vance, who had been longest in the area, said he thought he knew of a downward-running track that would take them not immediately to Chambe, but at least near a large and well-established tea plantation at the foot of the massif on its eastern side. It bypassed most of the higher ridges they had already negotiated. His suggestion now was that he should set off in advance of the rest of the party and take the first opportunity available to him of making arrangements for transport back to base. He discussed the proposal with the native guide. The man grasped the situation and approved. He remembered this alternate track, and felt confident that he could lead the bearers down along it and get them safely off the mountain. Certainly the Bwana should go ahead—he would be able to travel faster than the others since he knew the track so well.

They broke camp at eight o'clock that morning. Richard Vance had departed ahead of the others, cheerful in spite of the icy, blinding deluge. Before he was twenty yards away, he had completely vanished behind the pall of driving rain that seemed and felt as solid and impenetrable as glass. No sooner had they started off behind him than the track began to become steeper and steeper with every hundred yards covered. It ran for a time along the right-hand side of a deep cleft that descended almost sheer into the terrible Ruo Gorge, one of the most spectacular in the whole of the Mlanje massif. At times it was so steep that the bearers had to lower themselves and their forty-pound loads a foot or two at a time, by hanging on to the roots of the cedars that had been exposed by having the soil around them washed clean away. Sometimes they had to shed their loads completely and form a human chain, handing each load downward from one man to the next, only to take up their burdens again when it was possible to stand without the risk of slipping down the cleft to be lost forever in its depths.

Louder even than the incessant scream of the wind and hiss of the driving rain were the waterfalls in the gorges and on the precipices alongside them, swollen suddenly and to gigantic volume by the advent of the Chiperone. The track now passed along the sheer side of a precipice, clinging to it like a narrow ribbon in danger at every moment of being snapped by the weight imposed upon it. Down each precipice, made all the more sinister by the blackness of the rock composing it, tumbled these snow-white cascades of water—thousands of tons of foaming water dropping sheer for two, three, even four thousand feet. Its weight seemed to shake the ground on which they walked.

Then, after perhaps three or four hours of this sliding, treacherous descent, the track unexpectedly leveled out and widened appreciably. But it still ran along the edge of this great cleft in the mountainside. They swung around a bend and were surprised to find Richard Vance sitting on a boulder on the very edge of a swiftly flowing stream. He was unconcernedly constructing what the natives referred to as a "monkey rope"—a rope composed of lengths of the supple creeper that flourished there and knotted firmly together.

He explained what was of course obvious when they had gotten over their surprise at finding him there, that it was necessary to cross this stream. Ordinarily, this did not present much of a problem, so long as you knew where the steadiest boulders lay in its bed. However, with the stream swollen to its present proportions, he did not feel prepared to risk the crossing unless he had a noose of rope around his waist and someone to hold the other end of it—just in case he missed his footing.

The rest of the party halted and contemplated the stream, which was now more a stretch of rapids than merely flowing water between two banks. It emerged from a deep cleft high above them and fell steeply to break up on a scatter of tumbled boulders. Then it ran comparatively smoothly for perhaps twenty or twenty-five yards, before falling suddenly over a ledge and down into the main Ruo Gorge. The noise of the waterfall above them, and of the one below them, was so tremendous that they could only make each other understand what they were saying by mouthing their words and making explanatory gestures. The ground beneath their feet vibrated with the fury of the tumbling water. Even though there were trees all about them, the wind was so powerful that it swept the rain like a legion of devils among the tree trunks and swaying lianas, icy shafts, bitter and menacing. Now that the men had stopped their strenuous walking for the moment, the cold struck at their very bones.

Van der Post decided to survey the edge of the stream in order to see whether he could find a more promising point at which the attempt at the crossing might be made. When he returned, he found Quillan trying to light a fire. The native bearers had gone into a huddle, and it looked as though, for all their assumed loyalty, they were now contemplating mutiny. They were thinly clad, and obviously suffering even more from the cold than the white men. Only two years ago, Quillan told the others, two hard-bitten foresters had died on this very spot from exposure during a five-day onslaught of the Chiperone. If only he could get a fire going, it might put fresh heart into these wretched men, who were evidently very near the end of their tether.

While Quillan worked on the fire, coaxing it into a blaze in spite of the dampness of the available fuel, van der Post took a closer look at the monkey-rope Vance had been fabricating. He did not like the looks of it at all. Though lianas are tough, they can be treacherous, and to tie a reliable knot in them is very difficult indeed. For a man to trust himself to such a rope, when exposed to the strength of so swift and remorseless a current, would be to invite disaster.

He remembered that among the innumerable items of equipment with which the carriers had been loaded there were two good lengths of manilla rope. He located these, knotted them together himself, and then got four men to haul on the completed rope in order to test it for strength and the security of the knot. It held admirably, and though he examined the knot carefully, there was no sign of its having given an inch.

So, he fixed to one end of the rope a pair of hide straps from one of the haversacks, forming them into a sort of harness that could be slipped over a man's chest in order to hold him safely. For all that, he did not feel happy about permitting young Richard Vance to risk this hazardous crossing. He reminded himself that he was responsible for this expedition, even though it had been ordered by the British Government and two of its officials were with him. He had no right, moral or otherwise, to permit someone else to undertake so risky an enterprise. It was better that he, as leader, should undertake it himself. He put the point firmly to Quillan and Vance.

But Richard Vance pointed out to him, with absolute logic, that he was the only man who had ever made this passage across the stream. Admittedly he had done it only when the flow of water was comparatively slight. But he had crossed at this very point more than once, and was confident that he knew exactly where each firm boulder would be found to offer him a foothold in midstream, even though it might be covered by water. Van der Post knew at heart that what he said was reasonable. At the same time, like any conscientious leader of an expedition, he was unhappy at allowing a member of his party to undertake something which he felt he should attempt himself.

Well secured in his harness, therefore, Richard Vance approached the near bank. As much as anything, he said, he wanted to cross to the far side so that he could rapidly obtain help for the native bearers shivering around the fire and so obviously in distress. They were men he knew, men from the district under his care, and he felt for them. With help from the men on the tea plantation he could quickly return, and soon the whole party would be able to use the transport he would find there. Though he had not been very long in Nyasaland, he had developed a deep and very real affection for these natives, so cheerful and willing in general, and so loyal to their employers.

Van der Post offered some advice, out of his own long experience. He told Vance to keep his face turned upstream, never to turn away and look downstream, and to lean his weight against the thrust of the water, even at the risk of plunging into it. Even that, he pointed out, would be better than to remain upright and be swept out of balance by its force. Meanwhile Quillan had cut him a stout stick, and urged him never to place his foot forward beneath the water until he had tested the stream bed with it and ascertained where his foot would fall.

Richard Vance grinned. He would be all right, he said. He had done this crossing before, and was pretty surefooted. But van der Post and Quillan were taking no chances. They knotted the free end of the rope so that it would not pull through their hands. Then they braced their feet against the root of a tree near the riverbank, and prepared to pay out the rope a foot at a time, or even by inches only, as their young companion worked his way across to the farther bank.

He slithered down the near bank and entered the water— thigh deep, first, and then nearly to his waist as he took a few cautious steps away from his starting point. Van der Post was relieved to note that the water appeared to get no deeper as he advanced toward the middle of the stream. Either Vance was locating, with very great skill, each successive boulder in the stream bed and stepping from it to the next or in fact the stream was not deep here at all, even though it was swollen by mountain torrents and flowing so rapidly. He began to breathe more easily.

Then, suddenly, unexpectedly, there was trouble. Anxiously watching from his position on the bank, van der Post was horrified to see Vance turn about and face downstream —the very action he had been so strictly warned against. He and Quillan could see the weight of the water building up against his back, causing him to bend over. A moment later, to their astonishment, they saw Vance jettison the stick Quillan had cut for him. It fell onto the water, and shot away downstream like an arrow released from a longbow.

The next moment, above the tumult of the water, the hissing of the rain and the scream of the Chiperone, they heard Vance cry, "More rope!" They could not believe their ears. The whole object of the rope was to serve as a safeguard, to hold the man, if necessary, against the brutal pull of the stream. And now he was shouting to them to loose their hold on him, or at least to give him freedom of movement! Before they could answer him, either by telling him they would do no such thing, or by acceding to his unexpected demand, the decision was taken out of their hands. Richard Vance suddenly threw himself onto the surface of the stream and began to swim with a strenuous but clumsy breaststroke.

He might as well have simply patted the surface of the water. There was unseen but formidable power even in the surface. The current picked him up like a leaf and swept him in a moment downstream to the point where the next waterfall had come into being. Here the stream tumbled over a jagged ledge that looked as though a cataract of black rocks had been frozen into immobility. Richard Vance's arms flailed as he came nearer and nearer to the ledge, but they brought him no nearer to the safety of the opposite bank.

Horrified, Quillan and van der Post hung onto their end of the rope, thrusting their feet hard against the tree roots in a desperate attempt to pull toward them the man now struggling impotently in the pitiless water. Two of the native bearers came to their aid, bending their lightweight strength to the hopeless task of matching the power of that current. The rope came as taut as a bowstring and drops of water flicked off it from where it had dipped into the stream. But by now Vance's body had disappeared over the first shelf of the rock-cataract for which it had been heading. The weight of water descending on it must have been shattering —not a deadweight, but weight with power and motion behind it. Even in the agonizing moment of helplessness, van der Post had time to speculate as to whether the rope would hold, or whether it would be chafed by friction against some sharp edge of unseen rock. In that case, under such tension, it must inevitably snap like thread.

Then a strange thing happened. By some quirk of the flow of water, the body, no longer visible, was swung back from near the opposite bank toward the near one. There was just a chance, then, that by this freak action Vance might be washed back to safety. If he had survived the battering, and not already been drowned, they would be able to get him out alive.

Van der Post called for two more of the bearers to join the others, and handed over his end of the rope. Now he worked his way downstream, watching out of the corner of his eye for any new movement of the taut rope that was still attached to Vance's body, presumably dangling over the far side of the rock ledge. He could not, of course, see him, but he knew from the slant of the rope roughly where he must be. There was just the slenderest chance that he might reach him in time. Just that tiny chance . . .

He came to within a few yards of the ledge over which the tempestuous mass of water was flowing. He came within sight of Vance, still harnessed to the rope and completely at the mercy of the raging torrent. He came practically within reach of him. He lay down on the bank and stretched out an arm in an attempt to grasp him—by his clothes, his harness, an arm, his hair, anything that would give him a hold and enable him by some miracle to haul him to safety.

And then—it happened. At that very moment, the tension on the rope proved too much for it. It had been partly chafed through by the jagged edge of rock. Even as van der Post reached out a clutching hand, the rope snapped and the body plunged down the cataract, to vanish completely in the water-filled darkness beneath the trees. He could not know whether, up to that moment, Vance had been alive or dead. But now there was no possible doubt.

The shock of Richard Vance's sudden and terrible death affected the whole party. The native carriers, shivering and moaning with the cold in spite of the fire that Quillan had built for them, were shocked into silence. It looked to the two white men as though the expedition might disintegrate entirely. There seemed to be no more cohesion among them. Someone must take command, and act promptly. Above all, the whole party must get away from this terrible place, and with the least possible delay. So long as they remained here they would only become more and more disorganized. The situation could even degenerate into mutiny.

Van der Post acted quickly. He commanded the bearers to drop their loads and start back up the mountain track once more, away from the terrible stream and the tragedy it had brought about. Having seen what power it possessed, there was certainly no hope of making the crossing themselves, even though in union there is said to be strength. So, they must find a new route back to Chambe, and leave the later stages of this expedition to some more propitious date.

He tried hard to rally the men, but without success. They were sunk in gloom. They had seen the white man drown. They were frightened by what they had seen, and convinced that if such a thing could happen to the all-powerful white man, then disasters even worse would surely strike at them. So, they continued to cower around the fire, unresponsive, inert.

Then van der Post had a bright idea. If these men could be excited in some way, he told himself, they might well change their attitude entirely. If each man among them were now to be presented with the reward promised to him before he set out, this should put him in good heart. And if to those gifts, already promised, others were to be added, then they would surely find their strength and courage renewed.

He talked it over with Quillan, who agreed absolutely with the idea. So, they ransacked the baggage, and produced a wide variety of garments that were their own, including some that had belonged to Richard Vance. Bush shirts and tennis shirts, brightly-striped pajamas, woolen sweaters—these and many other articles were distributed at random among the bearers. The men snatched excitedly at them, and lost no time in decking themselves in the most improbable assortment of clothing. The whole atmosphere changed in the most remarkable fashion.

Quillan and van der Post seized the moment to encourage them to start back up the trail. They responded so cheerfully and with such alacrity that it was hard to believe that they were the same men. They snatched up their loads as though they now weighed less than nothing. There was no question any more of leaving them on the ground.

Miraculously, they found their way back to the camp they had established only the previous night, and took possession of it again. The makeshift huts they had used seemed to have stood up remarkably well to the long day's downpour and the fury of the wind. Though they had marched more than twenty arduous miles that day over some of the toughest and most exacting stretches in the whole of the Mlanje massif, and had witnessed the horrors of Richard

Vance's death, the whole party slept that night as though drugged.

When they awoke the next morning there seemed to be signs that the Chiperone had now almost blown itself out. There was still wind, rain, but its intensity had lessened appreciably, and continued to lessen as they went about the business of preparing a morning meal. They faced a new day, but in conditions that were supportable. There was clear evidence that fair weather would soon take the place of the grim conditions which they had had to endure for so long.

Knowing that they were now bound for their base at Chambe once more, the native bearers stepped out briskly and with light hearts, a motley collection of men wearing garments that would astonish their fellows, they well knew, on their arrival. Their services were almost at an end, and their official payment was soon to come. Only two men in the whole party marched those final stages with heavy hearts: Laurens van der Post and Peter Quillan. To them, when they reached Chambe, would fall the melancholy task of telling Richard Vance's wife the tragic news of her young husband's death in the Ruo Gorge, high on the Mlanje massif.

One objective of van der Post's survey of the Mlanje massif had been to ascertain whether any area of it might prove suitable for growing foodstuffs or rearing cattle, for it had long been realized that areas of potential food supplies the world over were insufficient to sustain an ever-expanding world population.

The Mlanje expedition certainly succeeded in answering the question. Though there were tea plantations at the foot of the massif on its eastern side—the one, for example, to which the ill-fated Richard Vance had been making his lonely way when tragedy struck—it had swiftly become evident that terrain as wild as this offered no prospects whatever for the production of any kind of food. Cedars, yes; but cereal crops or cattle rearing: an emphatic No! Even if the soil had been of the right kind, the prevailing climatic conditions would have made the tilling of the soil, the planting and harvesting of grain, even the pasturing of cattle, quite out of the question.

As it turned out, the terrible Chiperone that had brought the whole expedition to the brink of disaster and cost one brave man his life, did not completely blow itself out for five more weeks. With a mixture of horror and gratitude, van der Post realized that if he had not gotten his party down off the massif when he did, it was almost certain that not a man of them would have survived the pitiless weather.

In his official report back to the British Government he made this point emphatically clear: there was no future in the Mlanje massif, save in the growing of its magnificent cedars. He was therefore commissioned, while still in the area, to make a second survey. This time it was to be a survey of a vast plateau located some six hundred miles to the north of Mlanje on the west side of the northern end of Lake Nyasa, in the extreme north of the territory we know today as Malawi. Like the Mlanje massif, it had only been surveyed from the air. Its sides rose, often precipitously, to some eight thousand feet, to form a plateau. From this plateau some isolated peaks rose to nearly nine thousand feet, but there seemed to be some steppe land between them, and this, the British Government hoped, might offer good grazing for cattle.

To survey such an area offered just the type of challenge that had always appealed to Laurens van der Post. As soon as he had sufficiently recovered from his grim ordeal in the Mlanje massif he therefore set off on a six hundred-mile trek northward, the second strenuous mission he was to undertake in one year.